# The Caliph and the Ayatollah

## Our world under siege

**Fiamma Nirenstein**

Translated by Amy K. Rosenthal

Published by ISGAP
165 East 56th Street, 2nd Floor
New York, New York 10022
Phone: (212) 230-1840
Fax: (212) 230-1842
www.isgap.org

ISBN 978-17-17-08952-6

*The Caliph and the Ayatollah: Our world under siege*
© 2018 Fiamma Nirenstein and ISGAP

First published as
*Il Califfo e l'Ayatollah. Assedio al nostro mondo*
© 2015 Mondadori Libri S.p.A, Milano



The Institute for the Study of Global Antisemitism and Policy (ISGAP) is dedicated to the academic study of antisemitism and others forms of prejudice. The opinions expressed in this work are those of the author and do not necessarily reflect the views of ISGAP, its officers, or the members of its boards.

*With affection, admiration, and gratitude
to Professor Bernard Lewis, thanks to whom I've had the good
fortune to learn how much wisdom and courage are needed in
order to understand the complexities of the Middle East.*

THE CALIPH AND THE AYATOLLAH
OUR WORLD UNDER SIEGE

# Contents

# Introduction to the English Edition

JUST OVER TWO YEARS have passed since I wrote this book. Not a long period of time in the great scheme of things, perhaps, but an eternity for the Syrians who are still being massacred by opposing but equally ferocious forces, for the Iraqis living under ISIS's yoke, for the brave Iranian activists tortured in Evin, for the innocents dying of starvation in Yemen, for the families of the victims brutally murdered in Paris, Brussels, Berlin, Jerusalem, Istanbul, Stockholm, Barcelona…for all those, in other words, who continue to suffer because of the caliph, the ayatollah, and their vassals. Indeed, Sunni and Shiite murderous ideologies continue to thrive and claim victims in a cruel, endless game that shows no signs of abating.

At the same time, the geopolitical landscape has witnessed profound changes on multiple fronts.

In the free world, there is a new sheriff in town. To the surprise of many, the elegant, cultivated, progressive, and politically experienced Barack Obama was not replaced by his former Secretary of State, Hillary Clinton, but by his very nemesis—a flamboyant, politically incorrect, conservative parvenu named Donald Trump. Inasmuch as Obama represented the liberal icon *par excellence*, the post-American president who broke with Bush's arrogance in foreign policy and provided all Americans with health coverage, Donald Trump was immediately singled out by the liberals—surprised and wounded by their own defeat—as the perfect champion of populism and selfish capitalism.

In fact, the reality is much more complex than this, at least when it comes to Middle Eastern affairs. As I have written in this book, and as is even clearer now, Obama has proved to be quite far removed from the image of the long-sighted, wise statesman that he was awarded in popular culture, which earned him a Noble Peace Prize just a few months after his inauguration. His decision to pursue a rapprochement with the ayatollah even as democratic protesters were massacred and arrested in the streets of Tehran; his will to sign a nuclear deal with the regime no matter the cost; his proximity to the Muslim Brotherhood during the Arab Spring; his morally and strategically misguided "red line" in Syria (which he ultimately abandoned); his stubbornness in reiterating sanctimonious and detrimental clichés regarding the Israeli-Palestinian conflict: these few brush strokes draw a very distressing picture of Obama's legacy in the Middle East.

While it is still too early to pass judgment on his successor, we can surely say that Trump has rightly pointed at some of his predecessors' flaws vis-à-vis the region.

One of them is their failure to recognize Jerusalem as the capital of the State of Israel. And another is the Iranian deal, which Trump, speaking at the United Nations, has not hesitated to define as "an embarrassment to the United States," and which he has consequently called into question. On January 12, 2018, he issued a final 120-day ultimatum to "fix the deal's disastrous flaws, or the United States will withdraw."

Indeed, the Joint Comprehensive Plan of Action (JCPOA), which was much vaunted by Obama and the EU as a masterpiece of diplomacy that would radically improve the course of events and multilateral relations, has already revealed its many dangerous flaws, sadly confirming what I predicted in the original Italian edition of this book.

Although the International Atomic Energy Agency (IAEA) claims not to have detected any violations on the part of Tehran, intelligence reports from Germany leaked on Fox News report that, between 2015 and 2016, Iran allegedly carried out 173 attempts to purchase illicit material for its nuclear program—in clear violation of the JCPOA.

Even leaving aside these alleged violations, the Iran deal itself was riddled with problems of its own. The agreed 15-year reduction (not interruption) of the country's uranium enrichment program is clearly just the blink of an eye for a millenarist regime that thinks in terms of Allah's eternity. Furthermore, the agreement deliberately excluded key aspects of the regime's nefarious activities, including ballistic missile development, terrorism, imperialistic foreign aggression, and human rights violations. And these are the tools the regime is playing with, endangering the entire world.

Starting from the internal situation, the state of human rights in Iran remains terrible and is even worsening—in part as a result of the West's reduced attention to this issue. At the very end of 2017, popular revolts took place in several cities across Iran, fueled by the worsening economic situation, notwithstanding the lifting of sanctions. The media reported that several people had been killed (according to *Le Monde*, 25 people in few days) in clashes between protesters and the security forces, while hundreds were arrested and tortured. In 2016, according to Freedom House, Iran carried out its largest mass execution in years and launched a renewed crackdown on women's rights activists. Repression is continuing unabated against women, human rights defenders, journalists, lawyers, homosexuals, bloggers, artists, heretics—in other words against all those who are perceived as a threat to the regime and its radical ideology for one reason or another. Amnesty International reports that hundreds of boys and girls have been arrested and flogged just for attending mixed-gender private parties that are deemed "socially perverse" and "un-Islamic." Thirty-five young men and women were sentenced to floggings of 99 lashes just for attending a graduation party. One journalist received a record number of 459 lashes for "spreading lies." Torture remains a shockingly routine way to extract confessions or simply punish captives in prison, while state-sanctioned inhuman punishments, including horrific practices such as public amputations of limbs and forced blindings, continue to be carried out relentlessly.

Can the world afford to turn a blind eye to this human rights nightmare for the sake of appeasing a ruthless regime, or should it push for a regime change that would free both Iranians and the rest of the world from the ayatollahs' grip?

Vis-à-vis the rest of the world, indeed, Iran is not behaving any better than it does toward its own citizens. Taking advantage of the terribly misguided decision not to include missile development in the JCPOA, Iran has carried out covert and overt ballistic experiments, sometimes proudly advertised in front of the entire world. According to a report by the Foundation for Defense of Democracies, as per January 2018 Iran had carried out 23 ballistic missile launches since the signing of the JCPOA. These included the launching of a Khorramshahr missile, which is capable of carrying nuclear warheads and reaching not only Israel but also NATO members in Eastern Europe, with its 2,000 km range capacity. This missile, apparently developed with North Korean assistance, has been secretly built in military installments that, as per the JCPOA, do not have to undergo international controls.

Such military maneuvers are not a mere propagandistic show-off: they are the corollary of Iran's armed imperialism in the Middle East, where Tehran is continuing to destabilize the region in a number of ways in order to expand its hegemony, taking advantage of the Syrian chaos and of ISIS's menace.

The JCPOA has provided Iran with a huge amount of money in terms of unfrozen foreign assets and oil exports, which the regime has largely employed to pursue its imperialistic agenda. Iran is now definitely the commander in chief of all Shiites in the area: not only Syrians, Lebanese, and Iraqis, but also Pakistanis and Afghans. It has deployed more than 70.000 forces in Syria, between the Iranian Revolutionary Guard Corps (IRGC), Hezbollah, and mercenaries, who are handsomely paid. This effort outnumbers by far the Syrian army itself, and will be seemingly paid back in the form of a permanent concession of Syrian naval and air-bases to Tehran.

This is why another move under consideration by the current American administration is to blacklist the powerful IRGC, which controls the vast majority of the internal economy and conducts military campaigns abroad. (Members of the IRGC are already flagged as terrorists by the State Department, but Trump's intention is to label the group as a whole.)

Besides its Syrian vassal—the brutal Assad regime that has massacred hundreds of thousands of its own people—Hezbollah has emerged as the real winner. Iranian assistance to the Lebanese Shiite militia, which had fallen drastically in 2014-2015, has now come back to the golden era of about $700 million to $800 million per year. Considering that Iranian financing accounts for about 70-80 percent of Hezbollah's budget, it is clear that the JCPOA had a huge indirect impact on a criminal organization destabilizing the whole region. It is not by chance that Hezbollah boasts to have stockpiled 100.000 missiles, and sources speak of secret weapons factories hidden in Lebanon and Syria and ready to be used in a war against Israel.

As a matter of fact, the expansion of the Shiite influence in the Middle East has worried not only Trump but also those Sunni powers that have resented America's overtures toward Iran during the Obama administration and now feel threatened by a reinvigorated Shiite power expanding into their backyard. This has brought about a Copernican revolution in the system of overt or covert alliances on the ground.

As a mark of the increasing intricacy of the Middle East, it is by now inaccurate to speak of Sunnis as a monolith: Qatar, albeit Sunni-Wahhabi just like Saudi Arabia, no longer fits very well in this family picture. Indeed, the Gulf is witnessing an acute diplomatic crisis within the Gulf Cooperation Council between Qatar, on one side, and Saudi Arabia, the United Arab Emirates (UAE), Bahrain and Egypt, on the other. The latter countries have suspended all diplomatic ties and imposed an embargo on the small but rich and powerful Emirate for several reasons. The embargoing states have accused Qatar of hosting and supporting multiple terrorist organizations and individuals—among which they include the notorious Muslim Brotherhood. Indeed, along with Turkey, Qatar remains the staunchest supporter of this Islamist organization, which Saudi Arabia, Egypt, and the UAE consider a mortal enemy, by hosting its main ideologues, financing the Brotherhood's activities worldwide, and harboring Hamas's headquarters outside Gaza. Besides the Brotherhood, Doha also provides safe haven to terrorist organizations and individuals belonging to Al-Qaeda and ISIS and other groups included on the UN's terror blacklists. Saudi Arabia and its allies have therefore demanded that Qatar suspend all support to the Muslim Brotherhood and hand over all terrorists harbored in its territory. Another bone of contention is the role of Al Jazeera, which is accused of functioning as a propaganda machine and a terrorist mouthpiece following Doha's diktats. Qatar is pursuing an eclectic foreign policy under which it participates in the Gulf Cooperation Council as a Sunni-Wahhabi country and plays host to the US largest military base in the Middle East but at the same time maintains close ties with Iran, including military and intelligence ones, which Saudi Arabia wants it to terminate.

This fracture in the Sunni front is just one of the shifting alliances in today's Middle East.

Another significant issue, especially in the long run, is that Israel has ceased to be the no. 1 enemy of Saudi Arabia and its cohorts, which now have a more urgent, common problem to address in the form of Tehran. This overlapping of strategic interests might even have positive repercussions in terms of the resumption of the peace talks between Israel and the Arab countries.

In Russia, Putin has been skillfully capitalizing on Obama's miscalculations, building a spider web of alliances and accords with powers that it would be euphemistic to define as "heterogeneous." Indeed, he has been able to maintain a network including Erdoğan, Assad, Israel, Egypt, and Iran, and has recently added a new player to his collection, namely Saudi Arabia, which has purchased the powerful S-400 missile system from Russia. In other words, the commander in chief of the Sunni block has entered into an important military deal with a key ally of his Shiite archenemy, whose troops have helped keep Assad on the throne while Saudi Arabia has been seeking to overthrow him throughout the Syrian civil war. Turkey, formally still a member of NATO, has bought the same missile system from Russia.

One more element has intervened to further complicate this already intricate picture: an historical referendum on the independence of Iraqi Kurdistan was held on September 25, 2017, despite threats from Iraq, Turkey, and Iran, as well as pressure from the United States. The referendum saw a strong turnout and a landslide victory for the supporters of independence, who received 93 percent of the vote. Israel was the first—and thus far only—state to unconditionally support an independent Kurdistan. While this should come as no surprise to many observers, considering the ties the Jewish state has maintained with the Kurds for decades and its moral sympathy toward a people deprived of a deserved homeland for too long—just like the Jews—it is still noteworthy that Israel took such a bold and explicit stance despite the sensitivity of the geopolitical situation. Another unexpected, albeit indirect, show of support for the Kurdish cause came from the same Putin who is staunchly allied with Turkey and Iran. The Russian president has refused to impose an embargo on Kurdistan, in spite of the pressure to do so. What must be noticed by all the civilized world and requires an immediate reaction is the incredible savagery that Turkey, under the leadership of its highly controversial president, Recep Tayyip Erdoğan, has demonstrated in response to the Kurds' struggle for autonomy, such as bombing and shooting civilians in Afrin. In this area, Erdoğan has found a natural alliance with his old enemy Bashar Assad.

This earthquake of shifting alliances and contradictory interests shows that the old lenses through which we once viewed and analyzed the Middle East have rapidly become blurred and inadequate to follow the course of events.

These dramatic changes must be seen in the light of a momentous element: the defeat on the ground, if not yet on the global battlefield of terrorism, of the Islamic State. During the past year, the caliph has suffered significant losses. After liberating Mosul, the Kurds and the Syrian Democratic Forces, backed by the West, have taken control of ISIS's de facto capital of Raqqa, while the Iraqi army has recaptured the city of Hawij. At the beginning of November 2017, ISIS also lost its final stronghold Deir Ezzor, close to the border with Iraq and rich in oil fields. The terror entity now controls just a tiny percentage of the territory it held at the height of its power.

While we must all celebrate the monster's near-defeat and rejoice on behalf of all the women stripping off their black prisons of cloth to finally show their colorful veils, the men who are no longer cannon fodder for the caliph, and the victims of horrible torture who have been released from their agony, we should at the same time be conscious of the price we have paid to achieve this success—and how much we still have to pay. The war is not over.

First, Assad is now stably back on his throne. Skillfully exploiting the threat posed by ISIS and thanks to the intervention of his Russian and Iranian allies, he has been able to reconquer most of his lost territory, including the key city of Aleppo, and is considered at this point to be the almost irrevocable winner of the Syrian civil war. This helps to explain why Turkey and Saudi Arabia view the alliance with Russia as being more important than an unlikely regime change.

Second, the great game is far from being over. ISIS has been defeated from two sides: on one side by Russia, Assad, and Hezbollah, and on the other side by the Kurds, with American support. As happened during the Second World War, the first priority was to fight the common enemy, but the next conflict between such heterogeneous forces already looms on the horizon. Assad would hardly renounce any part of Syria if he felt he had the strength to reconquer it all. But would the Syrian Kurds, who bore the most heroic part of the struggle against ISIS, quietly go back under Assad's yoke, especially now that the Kurdish national cause is enjoying some momentum? Similarly, the United States, which has contributed so much to ISIS's defeat in terms of intelligence and air force campaigns, is unlikely to accept the surrender of the fruit of its labors to Damascus, Moscow, and Tehran. Israel, on its part, cannot afford to have Iran and Hezbollah, armed to the teeth with conventional and chemical weapons, pressing on the Syrian and Lebanese borders, which is why over the past two years it has conducted nearly 100 air strikes against weapons convoys destined for Hezbollah and chemical weapons facilities. Putin's refusal to allow Israel an Iran- and Hezbollah-free buffer zone along its borders is certainly another element that does not bode well for the future.

In post-ISIS Iraq, the situation is no better. Are the Iraqi Kurds ready to quietly submit to Baghdad, as happened in Kirkuk, after having done the dirty work against ISIS in its stead? And what stance is the United States going to take vis-à-vis two key allies—both trained and armed by the United States—that are on the brink of starting a new civil war?

In all this chaos, two actors seem to have everything to gain: Russia and Iran. Indeed, the battle against ISIS earned Iran an entrenched presence not only in Syria but also in Iraq, where the ruthless IRGC led by General Suleimani now controls most of the liberated territory in coordination with the central government. This means that the Sunni population already tormented by ISIS now faces a Shiite threat, and we should be wary of the escalating sectarian tensions and their repercussions. On the one hand, the Sunni tribes could once again turn to jihadist groups, under whatever label, in order to get rid of the Iranians, following the established pattern. Analysts, indeed, view sectarian tensions as one of the main catalysts for Al-Qaeda's and ISIS's penetration in these territories. On the other hand, these tensions could become yet another trigger for mass migration to Europe, especially if the Shiites keep punishing and indiscriminately subjugating the Sunnis, whether terrorists or not.

In conclusion, we cannot fully rejoice in ISIS's retreat if it comes at the price of perpetuating the mistakes of the past, like when the West ignored some dangerous radicals just because they were opposed to other radicals. To avoid this, however, it must abandon its fears, reluctance, and short-sighted opportunism and reassume the protagonist's role in the struggle against Islamic extremism wherever it comes from, taking courageous decisions.

Europe, which is hesitant, toothless, and feeble, should address once and for all the radical monster lurking beneath its beautiful cities full of glorious history. In other words, it should tackle the Islamic radicalization thriving in its neighborhoods and the disaffected youngsters who love Sharia instead of our liberal constitutions, Sharia more than freedom, and death more than life, and are still listening to the sirens of the moribund caliphate. It has been a criminal mistake to turn a blind eye, in the name of a misguided multiculturalism, to the abuses committed against women, atheists, and homosexuals within Muslim communities living just next door to us. It has been a mortal mistake to think that terrorism and Islamism were two disconnected issues, empowering groups like the Muslim Brotherhood, or allowing Saudi Arabia, Kuwait, and Qatar to send radical preachers to spread hatred against our societies and our freedom. We have been paying for these errors with our blood, and it would be foolish to think that the struggle is over: the more ISIS loses grip on the ground, the more it will spread its poison in the West, and especially in Europe, which will now be subjected to hordes of returnees from the Iraqi and Syrian battlefields.

In any case, Europe can do little without the United States. It is up to America to resume the role it relinquished in the Middle East. International relations do not tolerate vacuums, and the U.S. retreat has resulted in the emergence of other powers that do not espouse our liberal democratic beliefs. The

United States is not merely one superpower among others: it remains a guiding light due to the principles it represents—whose only harbinger in the Middle East is Israel.

It is therefore of paramount importance that the free world take on, once again and with firm belief, the battle against the caliph and the ayatollah—and not let either prevail. We owe this to our liberal democratic heritage and to all those who are still looking at that heritage of liberty as the sole hope for a decent life.

*April 2018*

# Introduction

UNDAMENTAL VALUES: tolerance, humanity, and fraternity. In 1994, this was how Václav Havel described the European spirit in his call for a common "Charter." It was to be a "community of destiny," wrote the author, a dissident during the communist era and then president of the Czech Republic, and would realize the dream of Europe as a "Community of Life," an "Economic and Social Community," and a "Community of Responsibility," all marching together toward a common identity that would delineate man's destiny, the *Homo europaeus* that would bring peace to the world after so much suffering, the just man. It was an optimistic vision and one full of good intentions. However, this happened before the advent of the Visigoths and Huns, before the dreams of multiculturalism and of a reconciled Mediterranean—reciprocally complementary and integrated with trade, tourism, interreligious dialogue, and exchanges between cultures—had been lost in the sound of the waves crashing loudly on the miserable boats sinking in *Mare Nostrum*, in which thousands of innocent, hungry people are crammed, more desperate than the slaves transported during the eighteenth century with terrorized women and children to American shores, like meat for the market.

The Europe we dreamed of seemed possible before the convulsions of two continents, Asia and parts of Africa, had accumulated between a short stretch of sea and throughout the Middle East, with masses of outcasts in flight, no longer gripped solely by hunger but also by fear and by terrorism—a large-scale terrorism against soldiers and civilians, which has assumed previously unknown proportions, forms, and dimensions, born out of and organized through the wars of religion and caste that lead to the death, abduction, sale, and rape of thousands every day.

The practical alternatives that remain to a Europe that has been left in a state of confusion have very little to do with the principles upon which it was built. Today, the Old Continent finds itself needing to choose between letting its brothers die, human beings with two eyes and a mother just like the Italians or the French, without offering a hand to the victims, or else becoming prey to a confusing and dangerous barbarian invasion without rules. What happened to "tolerance, humanity, and fraternity"? On the one hand, there is ruthlessness, indifference, and subtle statements of pity, which never seem to result in any effective form of aid to the desperate. On the other, there is fear combined with the inability to respond with international solidarity, with solidarity even among European states, to the magnitude of a phenomenon that could threaten to sink the Old Continent within the coming decades. It must be the same uncomfortable sensation that was felt when the immortal Roman Empire began to crumble.

The multitudes herded together on the boat of "Charon the demon," and the immigrant trafficker who decides who will leave, who will stay behind, who will die, and who will live, represent only the surface of the situation that grips the Middle East, after the disastrous initiatives taken by Western policymakers. It is not just the Libyans—engrossed in a fatal war between rival factions—who are flocking to the shores of Libya in search of a passage by sea, from which they do not know if they will come out alive, but all of those terrorized who are fleeing the

Islamist war that cuts off heads, kidnaps and rapes women, kills children, and starves the already poor: Syrians, Tunisians, Yemenites, Jordanians, Palestinians, Lebanese, Egyptians, and Africans from the Ivory Coast, Mali, Nigeria, Ghana, Senegal…

The Middle East and Africa are taking their revenge for having been so misunderstood. Desperate people flee by boat, from the hinterland of what is now a habitual display of blood that overwhelms common sense: they all come from countries shaken by wars, massacres, and crises, but it is inconceivable that Europe could possibly absorb such a large number of refugees and immigrants without being devastated itself.

Through a chain of associations and projections, following the many photos (which inspired a double sentiment in Europeans of both compassion and fear) of the unbearable image of the pure, solitary tragedy of Aylan—the dead child, with his blue shorts, fleeing by sea—Europe's attitude changed: the Old Continent found itself impelled by the same waves that carried the refugees, in their reality. Thus, it has assumed an almost collective responsibility in accommodating refugees. Angela Merkel, who lived through the overthrow of communism as a German from the East, knows that the world sometimes crumbles between our hands, and that when it does you just have to try to avoid its moral, legal, and political ruin. The decision to place Germany, and therefore Europe, on the side of mercy is not a complete response, but it is the only possible one in the face of children dying in drift boats or in the war of ISIS and Hezbollah in Syria. A careful acceptance of refugees is a starting point on which, at least, the heart can rest for a moment. A moment of respite to reflect, dare, and seek a way out of the horrors of jihadism. The first thing necessary to beat its wickedness, however, is to clearly understand what it is.

The destitute struggling to come to Europe are leaving behind scenes not of military conflict but of madness, of slaughterers convinced of the magnificence of their actions, of Christians slayed en masse, of girls kidnapped, a new return to slavery after centuries, while new tyrants impose themselves and old tyrants, such as Assad in Syria or Khamenei in Iran, persist. Gangs of mercenaries from all over, Iranian, Lebanese Hezbollah, Egyptians, and Moroccans, or even Europeans and Americans, violently attack the people of Iraq and Syria, which in turn generates monstrous groups in support of another regime of terror, that of the caliphate.

Countries that sought a path after the revolutions of the "Arab Spring," such as Yemen or Iraq, are engulfed in the conflict between Iran and the Sunnis. Immense crowds of ragged refugees have dragged women and small children to the borders of Turkey and Jordan, while large areas of the Middle East are crossed by Humvees driven by raving madmen armed with Kalashnikovs who have redrawn the borders of the entire Middle East according to their own geography from fifteen hundred years ago, killing anyone who is not a Muslim and anyone, even Muslims, who is not a Sunni, and even those Sunnis who are not sufficiently religious in their eyes.

Is it any wonder that people are fleeing? Or that they are joining the war that is underway, whether out of enthusiasm or self-interest, and believe, as prescribed by their sacred texts and dictators, that it is also necessary to export this war to our home in order to transform us into subjects of their world, which is so much more just and ordered according to Allah's will? The number of refugees on the move and in camps is more than 14 million, the number of deaths at sea is now close to 30,000, and it appears that this year one million people will be moving in our direction.

The Shiite imam and Sunni sheikh are taking advantage of this desperate situation, and have contributed to generating terror, as can be seen in Syria, from where 900,000 refugees have already fled to Turkey, and in Iraq, where nearly two and a half million people have escaped from Allah's willing soldiers. Their imperialism is long-range: it looks first to the Middle East and then to us with desire. It infiltrates terrorists that—after they have been well-trained in Syria or among Hezbollah in Lebanon—organize themselves in Paris, Rome, Bulgaria, Latin America…a little bit all over and coming from everywhere.

This terrorism has a common thread: it identifies a single culprit to whom all evil is attributed, namely, the Western colonialist, exploitative, arrogant, degraded, with its young unbelievers and women who compete for male power, wear indecent clothes, and practice free love.

The desperate mass of refugees often unknowingly hide and protect the violent, concealing them from within as they make their way to the next war. Youths who have escaped death by fleeing and being dispersed, sometimes only by chance become terrorists ready for an honorable death in jihad; their relatives who live in Paris, Rome, and Amsterdam get pulled along into a whirlpool of faith and solidarity in religion, language, food, and the oppression of women.

This book, which observes what we are facing through a lens of analysis and not illusion, attempts to describe in real terms the risk we are running in the face of the collapse of the Middle East. Ultimately, it outlines, almost paradoxically, a concrete hope for peace, if only temporary, which we think is written in the current situation. We will see, in fact, how it is precisely from a scenario as tragic as the clash between Sunnis and Shiites that hope for new stability can arise. However, for this hope to become a reality for the West and for the Middle East, we—the Americans and Europeans who have taken the wrong steps for some time by projecting upon Middle Eastern societies an image of ourselves that has brought us to a misunderstanding of what was occurring, which has resulted in intensifying cultural and religious hostility, creating conflicts, and thus triggering their explosiveness—must be the first to change course.

We will discuss in depth the nature of ISIS and that of the other imminent danger, Shiite hegemony, practiced with great, even atomic, effort by Iran. We will turn to the past and present misunderstandings that prevent us from fighting and facing the risks, and lastly we will evaluate which scenario is realistic to imagine as a way forward.

The origin of the current situation is in 2010, when the "Arab Spring" exploded. The distant past of Muslims, punctuated by the great imperial successes of the Arabs and Ottomans, had become over the preceding century a distant memory of supremacy and domination. Dismembered by European powers, the Ottoman Empire had lost its place to states that wanted to mimic structures of nation and democracy deemed extraneous and almost blasphemous. Tribal strife and lust for power have left the Muslim world to the domain of despots who haven't allowed these societies, which are increasingly poorer despite the blessing of oil, to make any progress.

Arabs, and the Muslim world as a whole, have suffered not only an incomparable human disaster but also, in the words of the great Lebanese Orientalist Fouad Ajami, a moral embarrassment. The entire world, including even East Asia and Latin America, has made great progress in politics, science, education, and technology, while the Arabs have remained in the clutches of eccentric dictators like Gaddafi, or ambitious backstabbers like Mubarak, or cruel dynasties like those of the Alawite al-Assad family. Turning first toward fascism and then to socialism, the tyrants of the Arab and Islamic world held Islamists at bay by imprisoning, torturing, and censuring them while stripping the population of its food and hopes. Their children went to study in Europe or the United States;

the children of their friends found careers in government, accumulating wealth and stifling change. Then came the revolt.

The blast, as everyone will remember, was heard in Tunisia in December 2010. Actually, no, the story begins earlier, but it ended so badly that nobody wants to talk about it. In truth, we must remember it with admiration because it was perhaps the only authentic, conscious, and desperate spring. In 2009, the Iranian people went to the streets to be beaten by the Revolutionary Guards, the Pasdaran, who defended the election of Mahmoud Ahmadinejad, pet of the ayatollahs. The Iranians are a great people, who proudly remember their past and do not think the splendors of the Persian Empire have halted. In fact, they embrace modernity and would therefore deserve democracy, and—in reality—it is perhaps the only country in the Muslim world that could truly practice it. We will return to this point later.

Let's go back, however, to the Arab Spring and to Mohamed Bouazizi in Tunisia, who in 2010 set himself on fire to protest against the daily injustice, unbearable misery, and rage to which he was subjected. Inspired by his extreme act of revolt and protest against an unjust system, millions of his fellow countrymen took to the squares. The revolt became uncontrollable, and within days Ben Ali fled.

After Tunisia, it was Egypt's turn, which took the world stage with the indispensable and tenacious help of Al Jazeera, Qatar's astute, well-controlled TV network, which was enabled by and which has in turn enabled the Muslim Brotherhood. In Egypt, it transmitted with great erudition the news of those eighteen magnificent days in Tahrir Square, which became the symbol of the Arab masses that were protesting for freedom and justice, while behind the backs of the young people aspiring to a new world the Muslim Brotherhood was preparing not only its ascent but also the power to put into action an Islamic project. In the course of a few days, it was Mubarak's turn to leave the scene.

Then it passed to Yemen, for years on the brink of a civil war between tribes that make and break alliances, and to Bahrain, where however the Shiite majority was lying in wait, because the majority of those revolutions were Sunni. Then came Syria's turn: Bashar Assad attempted to repress the revolts with massacres, but the Islamist organizations took advantage of the anarchy, spreading like wildfire and dragging the entire country into a fundamentalist rage that is the epicenter of the present confusion.

There were many immediate signs of the true nature of these uprisings, which we completely ignored in our infinite ethnocentrism. We had, in fact, considered them in the same way as Western revolutions, or rather as if they had been taking place on a continent that for centuries, with mixed results, had operated on moral and philosophical grounds, on the grounds of institutions and public education, in a carnival of democracy.

We looked at the Arab Spring as our mirror: we mistook as a demand for democratization, reform, and freedom the profound indignation linked to more than a thousand years of continuous transition from one dictatorship to another, from one form of arrogance to another, without signs of even generous liberalism. But these were not democratic revolutions, aside from the weak, feeble voices of young people, intellectuals, and the middle class who dream of an Arab world in which democracy and freedom exist. In fact, people were tired and rightly offended by the arrogance of their regimes (and also of the entire world), by the lack of jobs and poverty, and they aimed to rid themselves of incompetent leaders and persecutors.

The state had reduced its people to starvation and exploited to its advantage the ethnic-religious conflict. It had used the structures that were supposed to protect public order as personal militias; law was non-existent, corruption and the accumulation of money by leaders was repugnant; the military establishment did not serve national interests but those of the men in power, almost like mafia leaders. Furthermore, those who over the years had dared to even think that anything would change had been forced to flee—if they had enough money and luck—or else had ended up in prison.

In the Ottoman Empire, sultans gathered to smoke and drink coffee together with the leaders of the *vilayet* (the administrative district) and corporations: each came with their own demands and protests, the consultations were friendly and direct, the perception of the common good evident although not predominant. On the other hand, the modern dictators did not bear any sign of this respect for the tribes and guilds. On the contrary, they showed no reverence for the clan, professions, authorities, and great families. To all this one must add, in order to understand the fury of the revolt, the perennial disapproval that had originated from the idea that Islam's decline had been caused by a wrongful detachment, which was the cause of all ills, from the true religion, from the true Islam, from the true strain of truth, of happiness, of power, and also under international domination.

Already Muhammad ibn Abd al-Wahhab had been successful in the eighteenth century when he had founded a movement calling for the revitalization of pure Islam, without foreign influences. Wahhabism became the official Islamic current of Saudi Arabia's strictest fundamentalists. However, it is the mixture of Islam and nationalism that makes Islamic purism the main ingredient that feeds anti-Western hatred.

Hassan al-Banna had fully realized this in the 1920s, when the British roamed Egypt to safeguard their interests in the Suez Canal and, along with other communities of Italians, French, Greeks, Armenians, and Jews, had imported foreign customs like bars, fashionable clothes, music, and art. In his view, all things Western, foreign, and impure had blinded the minds of the Egyptians to the point of making them forget "true Islam." Inspired by the Hanbali school, which promoted a kind of Islamic puritanism, al-Banna went on to create the Muslim Brotherhood.

Among his most zealous followers was also al-Sayyid Qutb, who in the years immediately following Nasser's revolution realized that the new regime, although anti-Western, was despotic and tyrannical. He thus theorized that only Islam with its laws and its Sharia can create a complete system of life, while secularism remains the worst influence practiced by the West on Islamic peoples, and the Jews remain their primary enemy. The Muslim Brotherhood were imprisoned and tortured, and their property confiscated, but they have resisted and have waited to come to the Europe of human rights, to the terrible and secular Western Europe, which they actually despised, with the purpose of establishing their general headquarters in London.

The great Middle East historian Bernard Lewis says that Islam has never stopped asking itself why such a downpour of trouble befell it after the fortune of many centuries of power. The answer has always been twofold: on one hand, blame for the abandonment of the faith and, on the other, the belief that the West had trampled upon and demeaned Islam and conspired against it. In Iran, this had already led, in 1979, to the arrival of the religious to power, who were determined to instill Ayatollah Khomeini's true Islam and hatred for the United States within the state. Throughout the rest of the Middle East, and in particular where it had power, the Muslim Brotherhood began to prepare a revolt of a particularly Sunni nature, which was certainly of a social nature, but was above all a cry for the recovery of identity against unbelieving tyrants and traitors to the West that had tormented those populations.

The rioters wiped them out one by one, except for Bashar Assad, who was supported by Iran with the brute force of Hezbollah, the Shiite Lebanese militia, which was armed to the teeth and had been founded in the 1980s with Iranian money to fight Israel. Syria had previously used Hezbollah to keep Lebanon under control, given that it had never considered it an independent state. Then, starting in 2003, it was Iran that wanted Hezbollah in Iraq in order to train Shiite militias, which they could send to fight against Westerners and Sunnis, albeit consolidating their own influence on the region. After the U.S. withdrawal from Iraq and the start of the Arab Spring uprisings, Hezbollah became increasingly present in Syria and later in Yemen, where it supports the Shiite Houthis against the Sunni regime.

It is worth recalling that the enthusiasm displayed by our journalists and leaders for the Arab Spring failed to recognize that Europe, in order to achieve democracy, had to go through five hundred years of authoritarianism and monarchy until religion lost its central role. Shortly before Muhammad Morsi, the leader of the Muslim Brotherhood, became a prime minister as eager to gain power for himself and his own as he was useless to Egypt's poor economy, Obama, along with many other Western leaders, said: "Now, ultimately the future of Egypt will be determined by the Egyptian people.... And I believe the Egyptian people want the same things that we all want—a better life for ourselves and our children, and a government that is fair and just and responsive." Yet, all around the world one could read the results offered by the Pew Research Center, always very reliable, which explained how, at the time, more than 60 percent of the Egyptian population wanted to institute Sharia law. It wasn't difficult to see that Morsi, the president-elect, was not exactly the democratic figure that people liked to imagine.

But the West did not take the effort to look, to thoroughly examine, not in Yemen or in Syria, let alone in Iran, the moderate factions that were not purely religious and sectarian. In Syria, the opposition was abandoned. In Iraq, after the noble attempt of the surge, American support that sought to help the country's population to react against the widespread ills of terrorism everywhere, found itself more comfortable pretending to believe in a confederal model that in reality put another dictator—Shiite rather than Sunni—in power. In Libya, the destruction of Gaddafi's regime led to the split between two rival governments and the powerful return of Al-Qaeda and ISIS, along with the addition of tribal gangs; Iranians in Yemen, along with their Houthi allies, lost the capital in January 2015 when Al-Qaeda attacked them with ISIS affiliates; in Lebanon Hezbollah, fighting with Assad in Syria on the orders of Iran, has taken on the role of the state, while its missile arsenal has become monstrous and threatens Israel every day that the ayatollahs need only give the order for an attack.

Five Arab states no longer exist: in each of them armed militias on both sides have taken power and destroy, for religious, tribal, or political reasons, adversaries—or what they perceive as adversaries—by forcing huge masses of the population to flee. From an era of dictatorial torpor, the Middle East has entered an era of chaos. Only the Kurds oppose ISIS with weapons, while Christians have become the favored targets of massacres and ethnic cleansing that claim victims in the thousands, as had occurred previously only in the period of the ancient Roman persecutions. The Kurds have a long and proud national history; they have been fighting for years for a state and to protect themselves from one tyrant or another. Christians, however, have no one to defend them. Certainly not the West, which seems to have little interest in the demise of Eastern Christianity. Just as it was also quick to forget what happened to the Eastern Jews, driven out of Arab countries with the establishment of the State of Israel.

The historic Islamic Empire, in its various forms, was never so cruel as to induce the faithful to throw their travel companions overboard, to drown them, out of desperation just because they weren't Muslims, as happened to the twelve Christians from West Africa who departed from Libya on April 14, 2015, and were thrown into the sea by other exiles, now under investigation in Italy; nor to align believers of different faiths on the seafront and behead them upon a nod from the commander, as seen in a video from February 15, 2015, which shows the mass beheading of twenty-one Coptic Egyptians kidnapped three days earlier to take revenge, says ISIS, on the Church's hostility.

The Arab Spring uprisings have, in fact, opened the door to a wave of terrorism that scares to death first and foremost Muslims themselves and, second, endangers our lives. For the past six years, the United States has added twenty-one names to the list of foreign terrorist organizations, and all but one are radical Islamic groups. In 2013, it is estimated that 10,000 terrorist attacks were carried out with 18,000 victims; in 2014 it is about 145,000 attacks. Since the start of the Arab Spring, eleven terrorist organizations have been added to the U.S. list. It was then, in fact, that the power vacuum, the confusion, and also the dissolution of security apparatuses and the freedom regained by jihadist prisoners and those of the Muslim Brotherhood set in motion the tendency to bring the Islamist push for revolutions to extreme consequences. Ansar al-Sharia was born in Tunisia, Ansar Bayt al-Maqdis and the Mujahideen Shura Council in Egypt, Ansar al-Benghazi in Libya, Al-Nusra in Syria, Al-Qaeda grew stronger in Yemen, and, finally, in Iraq, the most biting of all organizations, ISIL or ISIS or IS.

What resurfaced then was the true geographical partition of the Middle East, which was not that of the lines drawn by the

Western powers, especially France and England, who with the Sykes–Picot Agreement of 1916 had drawn the sandy boundaries delimiting the nation-states of Iraq, Saudi Arabia, Jordan, Syria, Lebanon, and others, while the true inhabitants of the area were and remained subdivided between the Sunni, Shiite, and Kurdish tribes, the Alawites, Druze, Jews, Christians, and Yazidis.

Without dictators to stop them, rival tribes attacked one another, and religious groups fought one another in order to advance their rights. Syria and Iraq were the first to fall largely into the hands of the Islamic caliphate. ISIS operated with unexpected speed, showing a tendency toward success for reasons that we will explain later, and rapidly increased its wealth when it took over the Bank of Mosul and began to sell the oil from the wells that it gradually came to possess. It coined its currency in gold, silver, and copper so as to avoid dependence upon the international system, managed immediately to terrorize the Iraqi and Syrian armies, and imprisoned around ten million people within its new borders. We will examine ISIS later on. We anticipate here that, beyond combating on the ground, ISIS seeks to gain access to the largest amount of territory possible by using the influence of Islamic doctrine and by considering acts of terrorism as the best way to destabilize and subvert order both in Muslim lands and in our own. While it becomes, in fact, a dominant element in Middle Eastern politics, the use of terrorism and religious insurgency tied to the social discontent of immigrants and their children and grandchildren, in search of meaning for their lives, is solidifying the global aspiration of ISIS to a universal Islamic caliphate.

The conflict between Sunnis and Shiites triggered by the Arab Spring uprisings has literally resulted in an army of fanatics on one side, that of the Sunnis, and in a bomb on the other, that of the Shiites, as well as the desperation of the immense

Arab population, which by now wanders terrified throughout the Middle East and spreads its hunger and rage to the world. Fourteen million displaced persons and refugees already fill the camps in Lebanon, Jordan, and Turkey, and the chaos that towers above us is lit by terrorist explosions in all our capital cities, squares, schools, and supermarkets.

Terrorism has become the main wartime problem of our time, but we struggle to understand it. The brutality of such attacks, after the Second World War, is foreign to us; the idea of the utility of a hideous massacre on innocent victims is unfathomable to us. How can an indiscriminate attack on the crowd watching the Boston Marathon, on shoppers at a Kosher supermarket in Paris, on children at a school, be thought of, with a cause-and-effect relationship, as acts of warfare? Terrorism is a mystery to us. So strong is our uncertainty over its rationale and how to combat it that we were even unable to give it a definition sanctioned by the UN.

When we reflect upon the reasons for the attacks, on the unexplainable rage that destroys mothers and children at parks, friends at the bar, or pupils going to class, we think that we are dealing with passing psychopaths, with actions committed randomly, as Obama has said in reference to the attack, which was on the contrary very well planned, on the Hypercacher supermarket in Paris. We see terrorism as a series of random actions, phenomena related to states of psychosis that can be cured through dialogue, understanding, and, in the most political cases, through negotiation.

Nothing could be more misguided. What you will read in this book is how the combined stranglehold of the caliph and the ayatollah, which threatens to crush Europe and the United States, moves, so to speak, from very well-motivated and specific reasons; and how terrorist actions carried out throughout the world—for example, the massacre at the Jewish cultural center in Buenos Aires that in 1994, through Hezbollah, Iran took care to orchestrate, or that of Burgas in Bulgaria in 2012 against Israeli tourists, or, what's more, the 1996 bomb attack at the Khobar Towers, where foreign military personnel resided, in Saudi Arabia, or, passing to ISIS, the beheadings of Westerners and the mass slaughter of Shiites, the enslavement of Christian and Yazidi women, the crucifixions of enemies of the Islamic State, and the executions of homosexuals—are all part of cold-blooded planning that has been perfected over the years.

Massive attacks, starting with the Twin Towers, have always had a strategic plan behind them: in the case of Al-Qaeda, a strategy of world disorder that encourages distrust of Western power, weakens it and devalues it, makes us all bend to its will and, in the end, impels us to revolt, after thousands of exhausting checks at airports and in a state of constant fear, which make us feel like slaves to a status quo that has been determined not by us but by the will of others, powerful, pervasive, who have not yet come to power, but will. There is a very clear example in the ten bombs that exploded in Madrid on March 11, 2004, on the Cercanías rail network, resulting in 191 victims. Three days later, José María Aznar lost the election and José Luis Rodríguez Zapatero came to power. In response to the attacks, Zapatero decided to withdraw the Spanish troops from Iraq.

Islamic terrorism kills journalists, from Daniel Pearl to Steven Sotloff and James Foley, and here the reason is tied to the immense influence that the narrative of Islam as defeated and humiliated by the West has had on international public opinion. It's a storyline that, in the eyes of the cutthroats, can only be tarnished by corrupt special envoys of Western origin—sometimes Jews. While Al-Qaeda's strategic terrorism aimed to terrify "Jews and Crusaders" and to design the future of Islamic domination, ISIS instead begins with domestic, intra-Muslim terror, which helps to expand the controlled territory, because the organization's foremost goal is the establishment of the Islamic State. We will address this shortly.

Terrorists are neither a bunch of psychopaths nor a group of desperate individuals. Among the Palestinian women who have blown themselves up in order to massacre innocent Jews eating a pizza or strolling with their children, there were university students, independent middle-class girls. Wafa al-Bass, a Palestinian Arab resident of Gaza who was permitted to seek medical treatment at an Israeli hospital, tried to blow herself up as she entered Israel. Imprisoned, she was freed in a prisoner swap for the Israeli soldier Gilad Shalit, but upon returning home she immediately invited boys to become *shahid*, suicide martyrs according to Islam.

We live in an age in which terrorism has become a worldwide sickness. Terrorists are perfecting their techniques, acquiring over time increasingly greater expertise, and above all they are able to count on a new concept that didn't exist until a few years ago, thanks to which, with a kitchen knife, a car to send into a group of poor passersby, a stolen gun, and some bottled acid, they become participants, and protagonists, in a global movement of *shahid* assassins, the heroes of the nascent Islamic State.

Terrorism has worsened over time: from the Red Brigades to the Baader-Meinhof gang, which targeted individuals "guilty" of being enemies of the proletariat, it passed to the massacre terrorism of fascists who hit trains and crowds, and finally to Yasser Arafat, the true inventor of mass terrorism, who led his men to commit massacres upon unsuspecting air travelers or people standing in line at the airport, to implementing chain kidnappings, killings of innocent athletes at the Olympics in Munich in 1972, and the Entebbe hijacking in 1976, carried out in collaboration with the Baader-Meinhof group (Arafat often allied himself with radical leftist groups, including the Red

Brigades). In 1975, there was the hijacking of the *Achille Lauro*, where Leon Klinghoffer was killed in his wheelchair and then thrown into the sea; this was followed by the attack on the synagogue in Rome, in 1982, in which three-year-old Stefano Taché was killed and, in Turkey, another attack on a synagogue in 1986. It became fashionable to kill Jews: in 1994, at the Jewish cultural center in Buenos Aires, ninety-six people were murdered.

The continuous massacre of Jews around the world by Islamic terrorism, which seemed unthinkable after the Shoah, has instead become a leitmotif of our time. After the Second Intifada, there were attacks on a Jewish school in Toulouse in March 2012, at the Jewish Museum in Brussels in May 2014, and at the Hypercacher supermarket in Paris in January 2015.

Massacres of Christians are of the same nature, which became a monstrous habit with the murders of Boko Haram in Africa and the attacks on Coptic churches in Egypt in 2011. Included in this anti-Christian scenario are the one hundred Christians killed by a single blow in January 2014 in Nigeria and the attack on the Kenyan college in the Islamist massacre in February 2015. The list goes on: the murder of those who refused to take off their crosses, the attack on a Christian village in Pakistan in April 2011, after false accusations of desecrating the Quran, or the young believer burned alive in April 2015 in Lahore, the attacks on Christian villages in Syria, which began in 2013 in the village of Maaloula—where they still speak Aramaic—in which the inhabitants' throats were slit if they didn't renounce their faith.

This book explains how we are all threatened, how the danger is not random or caused perhaps by bad luck, but belongs to a plan that sees us as the enemy to defeat and a prey to devour. Can they succeed? Do we know how to combat this modern risk that has never before shown such force? Let's venture into its labyrinth.

# CHAPTER 1

## Objective: The Worldwide Caliphate

WHEN EVIL GAINS the upper hand, it is capable of conquering the world. Evil has a rapid and unpredictable impact on history, destroying all the efforts man has made throughout millennia to defeat the evil nature lurking in his heart. The fear of evil induces timidity, submission, and slavery. We worked for centuries just to suppress our thirst for blood and subjugation, to halt the desire to have slaves and shatter our adversaries, to stop killing each other with the greatest possible cruelty by seeking vengeance for nonexistent faults related to religion, ethnicity, eye shape, or skin color, in the name of which people were willing to slay their neighbors. Yet, when the demonic side of human nature unexpectedly rears its head like one of the gargoyles of Notre Dame, when it invades the front pages of our newspapers every day, the entire world and the culture upon which it is based are truly put into danger. This is how it is today: we are in danger.

The demonic force that drives one to kill has taken on a new form and is called the "worldwide caliphate." The terrorism of today, like that of Osama bin Laden, not only wants to kill and take revenge for old persecutions, but also wants permanent domination. In order to succeed, it uses cruelty in exquisite forms; it loves to publicize and does not hide its horrors, but instead it makes them the philosophy of our time, the key to converting others to its religion, and the guarantee that we will surrender. That will be the advent of the new world, and everyone will be happy in the order willed by Allah.

Because the nightmare that has been imposed on us by tens of thousands of men is so dangerous as to threaten the whole world, we will attempt to explain it here.

## Evil Has Already Been Stopped

It has happened on several occasions, even in recent times, that evil has appeared and threatened all or part of the human race. The Nazi atrocities of the twentieth century are just one example. In the Ravensbrück concentration camp, children were buried alive in front of their mothers; in Latvia, Lithuania, Belarus, and Ukraine, the SS or Wehrmacht squads forced men and women to dig the ditches into which they fell after being executed; women were made to strip, and photos of the gestures with which they covered their nudity in the cold or held a newborn close while being killed are an eternal cry of dignity against barbarism. At Babi Yar, a ravine in the forest near the Ukrainian capital of Kiev, 33,771 Jews were systematically exterminated in groups of ten.

What did the Nazis want? They sought to dominate the world. Why? Because they believed that by doing so they would have saved it from filth and contamination. Yet, why such cruelty? Because they thought fear would work in their favor and that ultimately their victory would demonstrate that their beliefs were right, much stronger than the civilization of which even Germany had been an eminent part; strong enough to legitimize the unleashing of those instincts that philosophy had hoped and worked for years to tame—we need only think of Kant's "Perpetual Peace." At a certain point the monsters were stopped by force, and in the interest of everyone. The monsters had to cease their massacres everywhere, although they had reached heights of great efficiency.

The Khmer Rouge in Cambodia similarly committed filthy crimes: three million innocent victims, with children who killed their parents by tying plastic bags over their heads, were also forced to participate in the genocide of the bourgeoisie and intellectuals (even wearing glasses merited being put to death). In 1994, Hutus massacred millions of Tutsi with machetes produced in China: they called them "cockroaches," insects to be eliminated. After months of propaganda, it took only a signal from a local radio station to trigger a genocide in which even women, children, and clergymen took part. Upon returning from the massacres, death squads reduced Tutsi women to sex slaves, preferring that those who raped them had AIDS so as to infect the hated race.

A few years later, in a war that spans centuries, Serbs massacred the Muslims of Srebrenica, peppering Sarajevo with sniper fire that took aim at pedestrians and detaining women in "rape camps." In 2007, hundreds of the much-hated Kikuyu of Kenya were killed during its elections. Angry crowds dragged men and women out of cars and stormed into homes, schools, and hospitals. If one's name sounded like it came from the wrong tribe or if documents cited the ethnicity of the owner, a death sentence was certain.

The Americans, the United Nations, the Vietnamese, NATO, we Italians ourselves…someone stopped evil. Someone saved us. Today, however, it is unclear who will save us from an attack that threatens our own civilization and lives. The unleashing of evil as a force of conquest required a precise and intelligent plan, a well-trained army, small arms and heavy weaponry, and the support of a fresh and powerful mass of individuals. It also relied on massive infiltration within our borders, even in homes in Rome, London, and Paris, as well as a carefully planned idea of taxation. Moreover, it envisioned how to proceed in the face of the pitiful weakness of our world, which consists of well-meaning but cowardly rules and of human rights, and which possesses remarkable confidence in its own elaboration of democracy, but fails to believe in the excellence of its civilization and thus lacks the deep conviction that we need to defend our homes and families that had been held by Winston Churchill and the Americans in the face of Nazism. Thanks to this conviction they won the war. Churchill wasn't afraid of promising "blood, tears, and sweat." He wasn't afraid to hate the enemy.

## The New Threat

Terrorism, in and of itself, isn't more dangerous than war: more are killed on the battlefield. Terrorism is monstrous, but that doesn't mean that it can undermine the structure of the society on which it pounces. I know something about this firsthand because I saw it in Israel during the Second Intifada. Every day a target was blown up by terrorists, death was in the streets, on buses, and in bars. The scenes of destruction, dismemberment, and rivers of blood didn't succeed in becoming a sense of threat for everyone personally, capable of taking away the courage of living and faith in human beings.

On the other hand, this is truly ISIS's great invention. The inhabitant of a Syrian village, the London office worker, the Parisian police officer, the Canadian soldier can all identify with the man on his knees whose throat is being cut. To see a head being cut off is much more disturbing than finding out that a bomb exploded in a café or even that subway passengers are lying among debris and blood. It is something that affects one personally because that neck belongs to you, it's yours, and you can't help but touch it so as to be sure it's still intact. The severed head resting on the breast of ISIS's victims presents you with overwhelming questions, and you don't know where to begin. You know, however, that you end up feeling utterly scared.

ISIS's atrocities are not ends in themselves. They have the aim of frightening me, you, and all of Islam's enemies, who are considered heretics, apostates, and infidels by the Sunni fundamentalists and followers of Abu Bakr al-Baghdadi, the self-proclaimed "caliph" of the Islamic State.

The massacres that, one by one, executed Shiites, poor Iraqi government employees, Christians, Yazidis, Syrian military, Sunnis deemed insufficiently Muslim, women, and children… sent large bands of soldiers running, which allowed the tremendous advancement of ISIS in Iraq and Syria; entire armies have fled, even Al-Qaeda terrorists have in large part surrendered. Then, from Iraq the terror spread to Syria and among populations along the Turkish border, among people in the mountains, in villages where even the mere idea of ISIS's black flag leaves them shivering in fear.

The promise of conquest, for us residents of London, Paris, Montreal, and Rome, and the caliphate's obsession with and determination to strike the Christian West become clear through a number of episodes summarized by a simple chapter of the Quran, which is inconceivable for us: "I am with you, so strengthen those who have believed. I will cast terror into the hearts of those who disbelieved, so strike [them] upon the necks and strike from them every fingertip!" (8:12). Sura 8, *al-Anfal,* is the sura of "The Spoils of War": it tells of the Battle of Badr, the first war against non-believers for the triumph of Allah over the entire world. To the infidels nothing remains but the flames of hell, whereas for Muslims it is not advisable to forge friendships with infidels because they bring corruption and disorder in the world (Sura 8:73).

Any one of us is a potential victim. The horror and astonishment of the soldier who was seized, in a random street in London on May 22, 2013, by two terrorists determined to behead him, and that of many other victims, as misfortunate as they are bewildered, can be repeated a thousand, ten thousand times. Lee Rigby, after having served in Afghanistan, Cyprus, and Germany, was stationed in London at the time. He was returning to his barracks when two assassins attacked and repeatedly stabbed him to death, attempting to decapitate him, amid the indifference of onlookers, in front of whom the two men proudly exhibited their act of revenge in the name of Muslims killed by British soldiers. The killers were English, both in their twenties, of Nigerian descent, born and raised in the Christian faith, who had converted to Islam and were proud warriors of the Islamic cause.

"Even if you are alone, hit when and how you can": a crowbar, knife, car, bottle of acid, any weapon will suffice. The message has been spread and repeated many times. Preventing these attacks is almost impossible.

In Syria and Iraq, only the Kurds—who in the course of their history have had to develop an exceptional capacity for resistance—have succeeded in defeating ISIS by expelling the cutthroats from some of the occupied villages. For example, in January 2015, they regained control of the city of Ayn al-Arab, demonstrating that fleeing is not necessary and that, on the contrary, victory is even possible. The battle resumed some time ago, through ISIS attempts to take back the city. They had already begun in October 2012, at the start of the Syrian civil war, to fight against Islamists in the city of Ras al-Ayn, which they liberated in mid-July 2013. They then formed a coalition against Al-Nusra, Al-Qaeda's Syrian faction, counting on more than 70,000 fighters. Women are also fighting alongside men and have managed to terrorize ISIS's warriors: a woman with her face exposed and wearing men's clothing, with a rifle in hand, is a blasphemy that succeeds in making Allah's fighters tremble. In November 2014, ISIS threatened Kurdish women soldiers by declaring that it would capture them and "marry them off" if they didn't lay down their arms, but the Peshmerga (whose name in Kurdish means "one who confronts death") promised to fight them even harder. The Kurds, who have always been persecuted by Arabs, Turks, and Iranians, are determined to finally carve out their state, and they refuse to allow ISIS to derail their efforts now that the crises in Iraq, Syria, and also parts of Turkey show the potential to turn their dream into reality.

However, can we Westerners, who are not even a little bit Kurdish, face the battle? We who have made the abomination of violence and war our banner, excluding them in our national statutes and those of the European Union and United Nations, how can we resolutely confront the decapitation of James Foley, the American journalist beheaded in August 2014, and the multitude of others who have suffered a fate that we would have imagined possible only for the victims of Aztecs, champions of creating pyramids of skulls, or, in more recent times, those of the Turks, who stacked the heads of Armenians along the streets?

Instead, however, there is Foley, kidnapped in November 2012 by jihadists, on his knees before Jihadi John, the executioner that, like in a low-budget horror film, somewhere between terrifying and ridiculous, points a small knife at us. The video clip was expensive because it must follow a Hollywood script meticulously studied by ISIS's production company: "Take one…take two," action, while the prisoner waits for his throat to be cut. They prepare a nice video for the masses, vivid, with the desert as a backdrop, menacing, but alluring on the computer screen, able to captivate and to convince a large number of people to join them—religious fanatics dazed by verses from the Quran, bastards, lunatics, frustrated individuals who haven't found a place in Western society, young people who don't understand what they are watching and think that they are seeing a film in which they finally have the chance to become actors.

Steven Sotloff, David Haines, Alan Henning, Peter Kassig, Huruna Yukawa, Kenji Goto Jogo…journalists who went to Syria in order to let the world know what was happening, humanitarian aid workers who distributed medicine and food to a population gripped between Assad and jihadists, poor youths beheaded after being forced to assume blame in the name of Western society, seen as enemies of Islam. The latter are ISIS's business card, packaged with the extraordinary participation of the executioner, Jihadi John, also known as Mohammed Emwazi, a twenty-seven-year-old Englishman born in Kuwait, with a degree in computer science from the University of Westminster and a promising career in high-tech. He's a veteran of several jihadist ventures in Tanzania, Holland, and Somalia, who, with his sparse little beard and small proletarian face, ends up becoming the official executioner of the caliphate.

It is evident that John, by doing everything himself, gets satisfaction out of being Executioner Number One. Anne Boleyn's executioner surely wasn't happy when he cut off her head, but John is, because he is stupid, with his stereotyped and impoverished British English accent. He likes to threaten President Obama and wield his knife, and he pledges "to descend on the streets of London." He performs poorly, Mohammed, but cuts heads like a true professional, pouncing on his victim like a pig or a lamb, sawing with gusto, while Foley does not scream, but emits a hiccup that should sound for us like a war cry, and which instead fills the world with profound, depressed anguish. We ourselves cannot believe our eyes.

## What ISIS Wants:
## Above All, Complete Allegiance to the Quran

This is exactly what ISIS wants, and its cruelty has two purposes. First, it serves to demonstrate that the rules of the Quran must be interpreted literally and that there are no humanitarian exemptions, following the Hanbalite Quranic tradition, whose offshoots include Salafis and Saudi Arabian Wahhabi—and which refuses any rational interpretation of the sacred text. The Islamic State will follow them exactly, and for this reason will conquer the world: this is the first message. While a shudder of disbelief was still sweeping the world following the burning of Muath al-Kaseasbeh, the Jordanian pilot, ISIS was spreading Quranic explanations: the video of the execution was entitled "Heal the hearts of believers," taken from Sura 9, Acts—*At-Tawbah* (The Repentance), which talks about how to treat nonbelievers, that is, to fight them "until Allah will punish them by your hands and bring them to disgrace" (9:14). Even though beheading is more common, burning at the stake is a penalty that Islam prescribes for traitors of the faith, such as those who convert to Christianity or fight against a Muslim community. It is a punishment that was practiced for centuries in various Islamic countries and abandoned only in the late period of the Ottoman Empire. There is a sura that allows you to do to the enemy what the enemy has done to you. Muath, with his airplane, in the squadron of the anti-ISIS coalition, had in fact spread fire on the caliphate and its people, according to the aforementioned explanation.

In reality, it was not solely about revenge, just as beheadings are neither simple responses to the refusal to pay the ransom demanded, nor are they a means to stop Obama's planes, as claimed by jihadists on camera. They are, instead, part of a strategy of terror that, step by step, has accompanied the conquest of a territory that by now comprises a large part of Iraq and Syria and threatens to annex part of Lebanon. In addition, it looks to Egypt from Libya, holds moderate Sunni countries under its whip, clashes on the ground with Iranian-inspired Shiites, and expands into Africa and Asia, whereby it promises the conquest of Rome, that is to say, of the West.

Every video has its own motivation, accompanied by a Quranic quotation: there, it was to incite Syrians to flee; here, for the Jordanian pilot, the choreography shows a squadron well-dressed for the occasion, frozen as they watch Allah's punishment inflicted on the poor wretch, so that King Abdullah of Jordan might call home the air teams who are helping the Americans in the coalition against ISIS.

It's no accident that a 16-minute video released on November 16, 2014, which cost at least $200,000 and required—one can only imagine with what further torment to the condemned—six hours of filming, shows twenty-two Syrian soldiers on their knees who are beheaded together, as in a musical, upon hearing the prearranged signal, with the jihadists who are this time—surprise—unmasked. Among them, there is also the young French convert to Islam, Maxime Hauchard. The title of the video is "In spite of the unbelievers," taken from Sura 61:8, *As-Saff* (The Ranks), which explains how Islam is the only religion that must prevail in the world, where there is no room for the lies of Christians and Jews. The videos are produced by Al-Hayat Media Center, the studio of the Islamic State, which also has an affiliate for non-Arab audiences, the Al-Itisaam Establishment for Media Production. The latter boasts of its numerous volunteers who zealously spread their messages in all of the world's languages.

The unmasked jihadists come from twenty-two countries, including France, Germany, England, Australia, and Belgium. If the fire for the Jordanian pilot represents the Quran and military power, the mass beheadings are a sign of discipline, power, and the willingness to commit any action, even that which is most contrary to one's culture of origin. In short, their cruelty is the mark of their total allegiance.

This is for the soldiers; there is something for everyone, though. Even the poor people must understand the lesson. For example, at the beginning of the war, in 2010, they offered us the video of the execution of a man for blasphemy in Raqqa, ISIS's capital. Who knows if he had listened to a song or looked at a woman or refused to kill someone? A Sharia court condemns him; he is dragged to the market square, while militants go door to door, excited about the occasion, calling people to come see. In particular, they invite children, who in fact formed a large crowd. A bearded man reads the sentence; affixed to the victim's back is a piece of paper that probably, as in the European Middle Ages, explains his crimes. Then the sword kills him in the middle of the square, as the crowd yells *Allah-u Akbar*, Allah is great. People of Raqqa, have you understood the lesson?

Assad's soldiers, or worse yet, the (by now few) Sunni rebel groups who still have not submitted and fight to destroy the regime, must watch the videos, hear the stories, perceive the stench of death, blood, and sweat, and act accordingly: "Obey, run, surrender, we are the future, we are the voice of God on earth, we are ISIS."

To be clear: the more crucial the clash, the more strategic the goal and the more we are forced to see displays of unthinkable cruelty, intended, according to a precise plan, as milestones on the road toward the universal caliphate. We must expect to see such horrors increasingly often, even at home, because we are among their declared targets.

## Terrorism as a Method of Conquest

Mosul and Tikrit are two important cities, both turning points in the conquest of the lands that today enables the caliphate to boast of a territory that already includes a large portion of Iraq and about 35 percent of Syria, a domain at least the size of Jordan, dotted with numerous oil wells.

Slaughterhouse: this is the word that characterizes the hold on the two cities at the beginning of June 2014. In Mosul, in four days, 1,000 jihadist insurgents managed to overpower 22,000 Iraqi soldiers, who had been moved onsite for the occasion in order to help the forces already stationed in the city. Leaving aside for a moment the widespread corruption among the officers and sectarian tensions between Sunnis, Shiites, Kurds, and Turkmens within the Iraqi army, the cause of its defeat should be attributed to the psychological impact of ISIS's ostentatious cruelty, filmed and spread on the Internet.

The caliph's men entered the city on pick-up trucks, shooting at anything that moved. As they advanced, and enemies were killed or fled, they took possession of weapons, artillery, and military vehicles: all American supplies that were provided to the Iraqi Army. The first to be slaughtered were Shiites within the Iraqi Army. They were crucified and burned alive on the hoods of Humvees, American military vehicles. Survivors of the decimated Iraqi Army tried to flee with little success: those who were recaptured suffered a horrible and exemplary end. Other soldiers united with the fundamentalists.

On the occasion of the taking of Mosul another massacre also took place, one with strong symbolic and ritual content in obedience to the dictates of the Quran. According to testimonies and evidence collected by Human Rights Watch, in fact, from the prison of Badoush, about ten kilometers from the city, about 1,500 prisoners, including Shiites, Kurds, Christians, and

Yazidis were picked up and taken by truck to the nearby desert. The prisoners were first separated according to ethnic and religious criteria—because the world knows full well that Islam is determined to eliminate infidels for what they are, and does not kill by mistake or by accident—and many Shiites tried to pass as Sunnis by providing fake names and citing false birthplaces. "If I find out that there is one Shiite among Sunnis, I'll cut off his head with this blade," one of the cutthroats would threaten. In fact, those discovered were killed a few days later. It was announced to the prisoners, who were without food or water for twenty-four hours, that they "will drink and eat in paradise." We are talking about more than 600 Shiites, and a few Kurds and Yazidis. All have their money, watches, rings, and documents seized. They are already dead. They are made to form a line along a small cliff. One after another they have to state out loud their number in the line. The killers are young; they consult one another on how to kill all those people. Initially they would like to decapitate them, later they think it would be more practical to shoot them. In the end, they opt to use a machine gun. Then they pass by the line again in order to check. "I rubbed the blood from my wound on my face so as to appear dead," said one of the survivors. Another wounded himself with a knife in order to deceive the jihadists. Yet another, when they placed a hot brand near his leg, didn't move in order to appear dead.

It was a crucial victory, like that of Tikrit, which was likewise completed with a massacre, that of Camp Speicher. We are now in the oil fields near Baghdad. The attack began on June 9, 2014. The conquest of the city took just a single, bloody day. Tikrit is a name that everyone knows well from the period of the wars against Saddam Hussein because it is a Sunni stronghold, the birthplace of the former dictator. Camp Speicher is an Iraqi air force base, which became the headquarters of

American troops in the U.S. Division–North and was later returned to the Iraqis.

The soldiers based at Camp Speicher become, after the capture of the city, a terrified prey, aware of being hunted: young recruits abandon their uniforms and flee. Hoping not to be identified, they run toward the desert or seek shelter in nearby villages. It's of no use. We have seen the horror stories in videos and heard about them from the few survivors. The trucks were loaded with soldiers, on some of which very young people can be seen as they grasp one another, aware of having arrived at their final hour. Cattle being brought to slaughter are certainly treated better than these prisoners, who were piled on top of each other, often suffocated to death by those above them.

Descending off the trucks, the homicidal fantasy becomes Cinemascope: a long yellow horizon, near the Tigris, becomes a line of human beings that march, each one leaning on the next as if in a children's game. They are the survivors of the first selection. Shiites were killed immediately in the bathrooms of the Kabin Zuhair school. Those doomed to die next now walk without daring to raise their heads; the executioners beat them when they try. The last thing each is allowed to see is the back of the person who will die before him. Once in front of the Tigris River, the condemned, lined up like schoolchildren, are given the same treatment once used by the Nazis when they executed partisans or when they massacred the Jews of Budapest by throwing them one by one into the Danube. Their march, offered to a worldwide audience, is over. From a dirt terrace that by now has become a bloody carpet, they are thrown into the river, the cradle of the earliest human civilizations, with a gunshot to the head. Downward into the Tigris River they go.

Shiites, Yazidis, Christians…it is the law for ISIS that they should all be eliminated: the Yazidis suffered a harsh siege, intended to starve them to death, in Singar, their "home." Two hundred children suffered this fate while women were raped and sold. The counterattack finally came from Kurdish warriors. Yazidis are an ancient religious group with claims to Gnostic and Zoroastrian traditions and an emphasis on the purity of the elements: air, earth, water, and fire. They can't eat vegetables grown in the land, for fear that they are contaminated, or spit or pour boiling water on the ground. They practice baptism and circumcision. They worship the angel Melik, in the form of a peacock, which they believe to have become the guardian of the earth after a long struggle and subsequent reconciliation with God. For this very reason, however, extremist Muslims believe that the peacock is Satan and call them "devil worshipers," worthy only of being exterminated. The same fate is reserved for Christians.

The endless massacre of the latter, killed like sheep at the slaughterhouse, has above all marked the conquest of Syria, where in some villages Aramaic, Jesus's language, was still spoken—by now it is necessary to use the past tense. This, too, is viewed as a sign of hatred for Assad's regime, which is not sufficiently hostile to Christians. "The regime can keep their Christians, but in the conquered zones there is no place for them according to the Quran," says ISIS with its actions.

Since the beginning of the Islamic State's venture in Raqqa, the capital, the *dhimma* system was instituted, or rather the law that allows Jews and Christians to survive in the Islamic world, as children of Abraham, provided they submit to certain rules: the *jizya*, which is the payment of a special tax on infidels, a compulsory piece of clothing that distinguishes them from Muslims, the ban on riding horses, the obligation to yield to others on the road, and other forms of harassment that have always resulted in great persecution, which could only be escaped through conversion to Islam. Sura 9:29 clearly states that "you will fight those who do not believe in God or in the Day of Judgment, and who do not consider forbidden that which has been forbidden…" and imposes death if they refuse submission to Sharia law, or conversion.

The Taliban have already reestablished the regime of *dhimma.* It has forced Hindus, along with the few Jews remaining, to wear a yellow piece of cloth on their shirt pockets so that everyone knows they are infidels. Hamas has also introduced the *jizya,* which is collected from Christians in Gaza.

ISIS does this in order to make its objective very obvious. Andrew White, the Episcopal vicar of Baghdad, tearfully recounts how four Christian children were forced by jihadists to recant their beliefs. After refusing by explaining that they couldn't stop loving Jesus because he had taught them since they were born, they were beheaded on the spot.

Jihadists call Christians "Crusaders." This is how they see them today, in a time of conflict with the West, and theirs is a vendetta that warns Rome—whose name is endlessly repeated in threats spread via the Internet—they are coming. Kidnappings, rapes, detentions of nuns and priests are continuous in the territory controlled by ISIS. After a thousand of these episodes, in February 2015, Islamists entered the village of Al Hasakah, on the border with Iraq, and carried away 150 Christians, all considered infidels, blasphemers, and traitors. A few days before, 23 Egyptian Coptic Christians were kidnapped in Libya and used, as already mentioned, in a magnificent display on the seashore, beheaded en masse.

It is a sign of territorial possession, like a rabid dog marking its territory, it is territorial greed that plans to annex Libya and Lebanon to the caliphate, and who knows what else. For example, it threatens Egypt by using Salafist groups and Bedouins in the Sinai and by utilizing the hinterland of Gaza.

Finally, there is the news that Boko Haram, from Nigeria, has sworn allegiance to ISIS by starting to behead its prisoners.

Not to mention the caliphate flags that wave now and again in Jerusalem and in the Palestinian territories, all Salafist. Even in Europe ISIS banners were brought to demonstrations at The Hague, when crowds were shouting against Israel, which, in the summer of 2014, was trying to stop the missiles of Hamas from raining down upon it.

If its allegiance, unwavering in the most ruthless cruelty, to the dictates of the Quran is, as has been said, the first reason why ISIS is sure to win, these episodes and a thousand more explain the second grounds on which this conviction is based: ISIS knows exactly where it wants to go and does so meticulously, methodically, with absolute determination. If it were not yet clear by following the map of the jihadist attacks, one intuits that Paris, Toulouse, London, Boston, Montreal, and Brussels are all already part of how the caliphate envisions itself in the world's future.

These horrors therefore mark the territory of the next Islamic State. In the following chapters we will see what it means to live in Raqqa, with Quranic rules that segregate women and brainwash the minds of children.

Yet we must not forget that while ISIS is expanding between Syria and Iraq, there is another Islamic state that has the same goals and the same strategies, and that poses an equally or more serious threat to our civilization. Only it is dressed like a Westerner and has a groomed beard. It doesn't cut off heads with knives, but instead it hangs, stones, and shoots. Moreover, it imposes an oppressive regime upon its citizens. As for the Middle East and the world, its project aims at the domination of Islam.

# CHAPTER 2

# ISIS:
## Where It Comes from and Where It's Going

IN SEPTEMBER 2014, Sheikh Abu Muhammad al-Adnani, ISIS's spokesman already known for his jihadist activities in Iraq, made a proclamation that all journalists, including myself, needed to write, given the new setting: al-Adnani asked every Muslim who resides in the West to choose their own infidel—an endless choice—and, in the absence of the possibility of waging war with ISIS on the Islamic State's terrain of conquest, to "smash his head with a stone," or to poison him, or to run him over with their car, and, finally, to "destroy his crop." What does this last suggestion have to do with others? It has to do with a lot, and even if you don't have a harvest, you will do well to consider it a personal threat. As Graeme Wood noted in the *Atlantic*, this is a very specific Quranic reference.

The communications company that sends al-Adnani's messages calls itself, in fact, Al-Furqan, a word of Aramaic origin meaning "the criterion," which is also the title of Sura 25, dedicated to unbelievers. Allah gave Muslims the Quran and "the criterion," that is, the ability of distinguishing good from bad, truth from falsehood. The sura vehemently preaches against unbelievers, who would only mock the Quranic message and battle against the superiority of Islamic truth. "We gave Moses the

Torah" (verse 35), but the fate of those who do not accept Allah is "total destruction": the unbelievers would live in a state of ignorance, falsehood, deceit, and conspiracy against the moral superiority and truth of Islam. Therefore, they, rather than us, should be combated, subjugated, and exterminated. Not surprisingly, the battle of Badr, which we have already mentioned, is also called the "day of furqan," because it is the first clash between Muslims and infidels, to whom Allah would have shown that the true religion is the criterion: if you accept it you are saved, if you want to live in a different way, you're dead. The history of Islam further dictates Muslim attitudes toward infidels.

Al-Adnani's message, entitled "Indeed Your Lord Is Ever Watchful," from verse 14 of Sura 89, *Al-Fajr* (The Dawn), reviews the destruction of all unfaithful peoples. After listing all Quranic references to them, always described as a bunch of liars and incurable enemies, al-Adnani instills courage in ISIS's soldiers, who despise the earthly life and whose ardor pours entirely into the defense of Allah and Islam under attack: "O soldiers of the Islamic State, prepare yourselves for the final attack of the Crusaders." He goes on prophesying that "we will conquer your Rome, break your crosses, and enslave your women . . . and if we do not reach that time, then our children and grandchildren will reach it." Obama, "the mule of the Jews," is vile; and John Kerry is an "old uncircumcised geezer." Finally, there is the promise to Europeans and Americans: "You will pay the price as you walk on your streets, turning right and left, fearing Muslims. You will not feel secure even in your bedrooms." Every sentence is not an invention but belongs to the Quranic tradition.

In fact, Muhammad, namely, the Prophet, urges not to touch water sources and crops unless Islam's armies are in a defensive position, in which case the Muslims living in the lands of the *kuffar* (the infidels) must act mercilessly and poison everything in their path. Al-Adnani doesn't therefore speak solely to those few unfortunate fools, hypnotized by a new cause after several personal misfortunes, whom we have seen acting with random weapons exactly as al-Adnani himself has suggested against Canadian infidels (remember the attack against two veterans hit by a car in 2014?) or against the "treacherous and filthy" French. With his quotes from the Quran, al-Adnani wanted to give a learned religious framework to terrorists' actions because it is fundamental for ISIS to recognize itself in the literal wording of the law.

## The War against the Infidels

In Islam there exists solely the war against infidels. If you do not understand this, if you imagine that ISIS simply wants power, conquest, and money, or if you believe that its men are an absurd gang of lunatics motivated by bloody impulses, swept up haphazardly throughout the four corners of the world…well, you're seriously mistaken. These are people convinced that they embody good in the battle against evil, the conflict between the *dar al-Islam*, the "land for peace," Muslims, and the *dar al-Harb*, the "land of war," ours. There is only war, war, and war for the infidels.

Pacts? Agreements? Truces? No way. This is not for Islam. When the Ottoman Empire, on January 26, 1699, was forced to sign a peace treaty with the Holy League, the famous Treaty of Karlowitz, and later had to give Azov to Russia, the most searing humiliation consisted in the fact that, for the first time, an Islamic empire had to come to terms with Western diplomacy, yielding to the will of the "Francs," a term that at the time was synonymous with European or Western for the Muslim world. It was a slippery and steep terrain, totally unsuited to Islam's warrior mentality.

There came a time when the Crusaders had stopped its triumphal march, but then the advance of Muslims started again with the fall of the Byzantine Empire and their entry into Europe. Once the Latin Empire of Constantinople fell, soon thereafter the Holy Roman Empire did as well. The world was fully aware, as seen in a thousand documents, of Islamic supremacy. Then defeats began, including the one at the hands of the Russians in the Russo–Turkish War (1768–74), which ended with the Treaty of Küçük Kaynarca of 1774. This event humiliated the Ottomans due to the territorial losses imposed on them and the recognition of the independence of the Crimea, ancient Turkish Muslim territory; however, it was the affirmation of the right of Russia to protect Orthodox Christians who lived in the Ottoman Empire that was felt as the first real defeat, the origin of the next disaster.

The compromises made with infidels, accepted henceforth as masters—and favored for their greater flexibility in trade and in transport and as experts for consultation—were then seen, in retrospect, as an affirmation of their own weakness, and an admission in their territory, even a psychological one, of Western taboos, which has brought nothing but misfortune and colonialism. Christians and Jews living in Islamic countries have always been considered a fifth column, a Trojan horse for Western domination.

Let's look to Iran (which we will discuss later), the first international sponsor of terrorism: a fundamentalist regime that hangs homosexuals, persecutes women and dissidents, and controls, like a true imperialist state, four capital cities in addition to their own. Its hegemonic war, today, is also an emanation of a millenarist Islam that wants to wait for the Day of Judgment. Indeed, former president Mahmoud Ahmadinejad did build a highway on the border near Samarra, in Iraq—where the twelfth descendant of Muhammad, the Mahdi, disappeared—that extends to Qom, where the Mahdi must come quickly and launch the path for the world's redemption.

For nobly Islamic purposes, Iran prepares the atomic bomb, which it will need in order to annihilate Israel and those who represent the *dar al-Harb*. But in the meantime, there is Iranian Foreign Minister Zarif, who reached a very beneficial agreement negotiating, day after day, with the United States and Europe, presenting himself Persian-style in a jacket and tie on the international scene. A photo shows him delivering a moving tribute at the tomb of Imad Mughniyah, the Hezbollah military leader killed in 2008, one of the worst terrorists in the world according to the United States and Israel, who has on his conscience hundreds if not thousands of innocent lives.

There are no jackets and ties within ISIS; they dress themselves in the same manner in which Muhammad dressed in the seventh century. They leave their beards unkempt—not like the Muslim Brotherhood, whose members take care in making themselves more acceptable to the West—and cover their head with turbans. They dress their women in long black sacks that don't even allow the disclosure of their eyes, and even their hands must be covered in gloves. For these movie extras, only violence exists.

What at first glance makes it almost impossible to understand who they are and what they want—these men disguised as if they were part of a medieval carnival, with long hair blowing in the wind, turbans and robes disheveled from battle, from riding horses or driving around on Humvees, where they are always perched with brandished Kalashnikovs—is our modern aversion to the past in its violent forms. We can't tolerate it, except occasionally at the cinema.

For us, for me, the past is wonderful: we make it our own when we offer gifts of its music or poetry, as well as when we view its architecture, paintings, and sculptures, because they speak to us about the everlasting traits of the human imagination. This is not the case when it embodies Black Death, a dog's life for the poor, arrogance on behalf of the rich, torture, and slaughter. We study that past and we criticize it in order to overcome it forever, because it is a kind of monstrous battle of Campaldino that, surging with Dante to the military clash *par excellence*, is never ending and fills the earth with corpses. But if we look to the past to build a better, freer, more just world, and perhaps regard it with nostalgia, others deem it to be the perfect and unalterable model of human society that gave us immutable rules to which the whole world must submit.

## The Apocalyptic Vision of Islamic Fundamentalism

ISIS, which wants to subjugate and behead us, offers a dark, empty past, where the only text is the Quran (I fear that *One Thousand and One Nights* has also been banned: too sexy; like many oriental poems, which need to be forgotten because they speak of "bad things," such as women and wine), where success in war is the only assurance of the purity of intent and guarantee of results. The knife to decapitate is considered a most noble instrument because the Quran prescribes cutting off the heads of one's enemies, and that is enough. Without forgiveness, modern temptations, and hesitation, ISIS truly intends to bring us back to the seventh century; it wants to live as then, to adapt to the laws of that time—considered perfect and immutable—and to get there it abides by precise rules written in the texts, which also define a foreseeable and forthcoming society.

In June 2014, at the now eliminated border between Iraq and Syria, ISIS militiamen were witnessed destroying border posts with bulldozers, while, with their fingers pointing to the sky, they shouted "Allah-u Akbar." It was a demonstration of the physical strength of a movement that within two years had conquered a territory as large as Great Britain, in an attempt to redraw a map artificially created at the beginning of the twentieth century. The same movement reflects a Middle East today pervaded with a pan-Islamic drive, which already battled against Western influences such as nationalism, democracy, and socialism.

This is how we must look at ISIS: as an apocalypse, looming over us in a technical sense. In fact, what Islamists propose is a movement that aims toward *Armageddon*, that wants to bring about the end of the world through its actions, and of course to get there according to the rules dictated by the Quran. These rules envision that this magnificent moment, which many of us would rather avoid, can only take place when the world has been completely converted to the one true religion, Islam. To achieve this, the world must be purified through the killing of numerous people. The Shiites (who number around 200 million), for example, who in their interpretation of Islam are considered apostates by Sunni ISIS, are all to be eliminated. As for Christians and Jews, we shall see: it depends on how ready they will be to submit.

In order to understand ISIS we must understand that the *takbir*, i.e., the expression *Allah-u Akbar*, Allah is great, is the way for sanctifying all that one does: when one says "Allah-u Akbar" while letting oneself be killed, or killing someone, one contributes to the salvation of the world. Even crucifixions, slavery, public floggings, heads on pikes, and mutilation dictated by Sharia contribute to the holiness of the actions of the true Muslim. This is why among the crowds gathered around the executions there is always someone who yells: "Takbir!" with a finger pointing to the sky. Immediately thereafter the cheering crowd shouts back: "Allah-u Akbar!"

The fact that this is how things stand for ISIS, but not in other areas of the Islamic world, means for al-Baghdadi's men that there has been a simple suspension of true Islam that only now is regaining its footing. "We will conquer your Rome, we will break your crosses, we will enslave your women," spokesmen like al-Adnani say. Their network repeats this incessantly: threats recur persistently, followed by a rejoicing *takbir*. "Allah-u Akbar." It is like drunken applause. There is no ostentation or celebration: it's faith.

Before the caliphate existed, experts explain, there was no need to apply all Sharia laws literally. Today, it is different. Since the caliphate has a territory, since the moment, in the summer of 2014, when Abu Bakr al-Baghdadi proclaimed himself caliph, many pages of the Quran that lay dormant while we fought our tiresome battle for human rights, have returned to life. Al-Baghdadi invokes Quranic legitimacy for the choice of his name, Abu Bakr, which replicates that of the first caliph, Abu Bakr al-Siddiq, the Truthful, father-in-law of the Prophet, who gave life to the dynasty of the first four caliphs, called the *Rashidun* (the virtuous). They consolidated the Islamic community by eliminating the apostles and by occupying the entire Arabic peninsula, attaching the then Sassanid Empire (Persian), which was Zoroastrian.

Abu Bakr is the caliph who will lead them to the battle of Dabiq, where, according to tradition, the final clash will take place, which will see Rome, or rather Istanbul, Washington, Paris, London, and whomever else suffer their final defeat, even if it will be difficult to get there. Now that the territory has been defined, Raqqa shall be its capital, and Abu Bakr, the caliph, and Muslims, after many years of confusions, distortions, and contaminations, have someplace to look in order to understand how their religion truly appears.

## The Marriage of Religion and Society

Attention: this is not only about religion but about a point of view that encompasses all the most hidden aspects of existence, from sex to politics to the way in which they wash their feet and pray. It also affects how they write laws, how traders should behave, how children are raised, and how to assist the poor.

ISIS militants love to boast about their public services and organization of charity: zakat, one of the five pillars of Islam, dictates giving a portion of one's riches to the poor. Besides this, there are guardians of the faith, who, if they find someone drinking a beer or smoking a cigarette, apprehend him, and the culprit is detained, whipped, and beaten. If you are unable to follow the rules or refuse to do so and don't know how to recite a prayer or a verse from the Quran, you are an infidel or an apostate, in which case the consequences will either be so harsh as to get you back on the right path or else lead you to a well-deserved death.

As a Jew, I do not find it difficult to imagine such a legalistic obsession. Religious Jews are similar sometimes: there are rules on how you should cut your nails to how you need to celebrate holidays. For example, *Shabbat*, the Sabbath, is regulated in a way that calling it meticulous would be an understatement: to reheat food or to make a phone call are terrible sins; the elevator, the television, the car, and a million other things that disrupt the very idea of a holy sabbatic inertia are prohibited on that day. Lately, a couple of friends gave me a lecture on the lawfulness for a husband to drive the car on Saturday in order to accompany his wife who is about to give birth to the hospital. On the way there, driving is permissible because of the risk to life underway, a circumstance that allows violating the rules of *Shabbat* by virtue of the sanctity of life. But once he leaves his wife at the hospital, can the husband drive back home? Apparently not, and in any case the issue is controversial.

However, you can be sure that, whatever the choice made by the hesitant husband, the man will be neither crucified nor sentenced to a number of lashes, nor even reeducated by force in prison. Even the strictest Orthodox Jews don't condemn anyone to death—even when a family member decides to abandon their way of life. There is great deal of sadness and anxiety toward a member of the community who decides to become secular or to enlist in the army. There might even be an excommunication, or perhaps they will prefer not to meet this person again; or instead, they might use every opportunity to try to convince this person to return to what they consider the right path. However, there is no rabbinical or secular court that imposes the death penalty or any other punishment upon someone for the way they have decided to live their life.

Instead, the Islamic State shall always follow, according to a scholarly interpretation of the law, its deadly punishments. The basic precept of creating statehood is always accompanied, in each new conquest, by the promise to kill, kill, and kill again. At the by now eliminated border between Syria and southern Iraq, a desert area in ISIS's hands, Islamic warriors will proudly bring you to see how the border of the colonial Sykes–Picot agreement no longer exists: "Behold, here is the new state." Then they stick a sword in the ground, where they run a line of demarcation, albeit wielding machine guns and promising immediately that a lot of blood will be shed in the fight against the omnipresent enemies of the new state.

Even when the jihadist tries to be kind, to explain himself, death, his or that of the enemy, is a refrain that accompanies the entire discourse. It is a continuous succession of "we will kill them, they will kill us, we will cut off their heads, we will smash everything, we will shatter them, we will triumph, we will conquer, we will happily be *shahids* [martyrs]," who don't dream of anything else except going to heaven to meet the famous seventy-two virgins waiting for each of them.

## Ideologues, Mentors, and Advisers

The parent of ISIS is, of course, Al-Qaeda, which was and is very different in its methodology and objectives. Bin Laden, who proved himself in the war against the Russians in Afghanistan, had come to the conclusion that the terrible imperialist enemy could eventually be defeated and ousted. This belief was transferred into his general theory, well explained in his "Letter to America," which he made public shortly after the September 11, 2001 attacks. His enemies were, as he said without anyone believing him except the great historian Bernard Lewis, "the Crusaders and the Jews," who attack Muslims in their lands, and—for him, who belonged to the Wahhabi branch of Sunni Islam, the most extremist Muslim that one can imagine—"the Shiites." While regarding the latter as enemies, Al-Qaeda was inspired by Khomeini-like Iranian terrorism and has also had contacts with Hezbollah. However, the historical hatred between Sunnis and Shiites ended the initial honeymoon soon after the first tensions in Iraq. Bin Laden wanted to attack and defeat the anti-Muslim order, namely, the imperialist-colonialist infidels, and he aspired to bring down, after the Soviet Union in Afghanistan, the United States as well. Unfortunately, he had some success with the attack on the Twin Towers, which started a chaotic mess from which we have never recovered.

His successor, Ayman al-Zawahiri, the Egyptian eye surgeon who currently leads Al-Qaeda, never wanted to affiliate with Abu Bakr al-Baghdadi, the Islamic State's self-proclaimed caliph. It is said that al-Zawahiri abhors their violence. It's not true. Judging by the leader's personality and Al-Qaeda's under-takings, which also include many beheadings, all that emerges is that he is a Qaedist leader: neither a man of ISIS nor a zealot of the Shiite world could tolerate that someone, especially in the same family, turns against him and challenges him.

However, al-Baghdadi's real mentor was Abu Musab al-Zarqawi, happily killed by the Americans in 2006. Al-Zarqawi did for a time lead Al-Qaeda in Iraq and established a doctrine of intra-Muslim hatred that hadn't existed during bin Laden's time. Al-Zarqawi first targeted Iraqi Shiites with a series of sui-cide attacks in mosques and markets, and he helped to organize other attacks in Jordan, Morocco, and Turkey. He then pro-ceeded to happily declare anyone he didn't like a *kafir*, that is, an apostate and therefore subject to execution: beyond drinkers or those with shaved beards, 200 million Shiites found them-selves in his sights.

This is perhaps the main legacy that ISIS received from al-Zarqawi's Al-Qaeda. The latter was then surpassed, swallowed, and mangled by the violence of the new group, but owes the education of most of its leadership to it. Education devoted to barbaric violence and hatred disguised as *pietas*.

Al-Baghdadi, al-Zarqawi, al-Zawahiri, bin Laden, and others are all disciples of Sayyid Qutb, the Egyptian Islamist ideologue who influenced Muslim Brotherhood extremism. His thought turned against secularism, dangerous Western contamination, and called for a return to the state of pre-Islamic ignorance, *jahiliyya*, a condition that only the perfection of Sharia can overcome. Qutb made political anti-Semitism a founding el-ement of contemporary Islamism and introduced the belief that the eradication of every non-Muslim element from Islamic society is the only path to peace.

The novelty of ISIS compared to Al-Qaeda, and the reason why it kills so many people every day, is that for them the main enemies of the Islamic State are *kuffar* Muslims, in other words, apostates; first and foremost, but not only, Shiites (Iran is a Shiite state, the only one at present among the Muslim countries). Bringing the conflict to the heart of Western states, Al-Qaeda had hoped to muster the Arab world's enthusiasm, and therefore to alienate them so strongly from their governments as to cause an Al-Qaeda revolution similar to that of Khomeini in Iran. ISIS instead directly strives to conquer territory in the Middle East, Africa, and the furthermost East; in the meantime it positions flags on our territory with its frequent attacks, galvanizing Muslims and its sympathizers around the world (and there are some, as impossible as it may seem!). The aim is always one and one only: to create a state. Its main enemies on the battlefield, therefore, are Muslims.

It is not paradoxical to state that, although Muslims are always complaining about the massacres committed by the colonialists against them, in reality Islamists themselves have carried out the worst massacres of Muslims.

A word of caution, however: it was not the will of God, or pure chance, that led to ISIS's rise, but the concurrence of unfortunate situations. The movement would not have developed if it had not had the opportunity to acquire so many experts and many weapons. Taking a step back in order to examine the Iran–Iraq War will help us greatly to understand the present.

## The Collapse of Saddam and the Sunni–Shiite Conflict

The Sunni–Shia conflict has continued for centuries, more and more dramatically, spreading to an increasingly vaster area and with a bigger scope: the whole Middle East and later the entire world, which both Sunni and Shia want to devour, each convinced of being the depository of true Islam, both persuaded that Islam is the only truth. We will see in the next chapter how this animosity, which arose at the time of the Prophet's death, has divided Islam.

At the end of the conflict with Iran, which lasted eight years, from 1980 to 1988, Saddam put aside his powerful officers, at that point dangerous for him, and formed Special Forces such as the famous Republican Guard and Fedayeen Saddam, the Nazi-inspired paramilitary organizations of the Baathist movement. They were experts in explosives and espionage and, as we later saw during the war, in the creation of huge mass graves.

After the American conquest and the dismantling of Saddam's regime, the United States designed a federal system, granting the Kurds an autonomous territory but essentially putting power in the hands of Shiites. When it became clear that the Americans had no intention of reinstating members of Saddam's regime, but planned instead to create a new "Nuremberg," Saddam's former generals, insulted and deprived of their role and pay, as well as threatened by trials, went underground and used their training to fight the new regime, entirely Shiite, wanted by the Americans.

When the Sunni insurgency against the U.S.-backed Shiite government was over, the Americans demanded that then Iraqi prime minister al-Maliki not only stop chasing down Saddam's Baathists but also allow them to return to a normal life in a nearly pacified Iraq. However, the Iranian Revolutionary Guards (with the support of the Iraqi prime minister and his Shiite entourage) saw a chance in the new Iraq to enlarge the Islamic Republic's sphere of influence on the pretext of protecting their Shiite brothers who for years had been harassed by Saddam. They continued to hunt down former Baathist officers, who found themselves persecuted, marginalized, and discriminated against by their own government. ISIS was thus able to tap into their anger and strength.

Today, it is precisely these former officers who constitute the backbone of ISIS's military force. This was the case, for example, with the head of ISIS's military council, Adnan al-Sweidawi, also known as Abu Ayman al-Iraqi, who was a loyal colonel in Iraq's air defense intelligence under Saddam Hussein. Despite his senior position within the ISIS hierarchy, very little is known about him. He has been referred to as a "shadowy persona." The group of former officers known as Jaysh Rijal al-Tariqa al-Naqshbandia, a jihadist organization that mixes pan-Arabism and the Naqshbandi Sufi school, is led by Izzat al-Douri, a high-ranking official of the Baath Party and Saddam's right arm, who appeared as the "king of clubs" in the famous deck of cards distributed by the Americans in order to publically denounce the regime's most prominent leaders.

So, the ancient war continues hand in hand with the new one. ISIS has been clever and forward-looking.

In the *Weekly Standard* of September 2014, Hussain Abdul-Hussain and Lee Smith wrote that the Arab tribes on both sides of the Syrian-Iraqi border are another key factor in the Sunni revolution led by ISIS: the map of the new caliphate, with the capital Raqqa and Deir al-Zor in Syria, and with Nineveh, the provinces of Anbar, Salaheddine, and Diyala in Iraq, overlaps an ancient tribal area of 435 square kilometers. Raqqa was torn from Assad's hands, even though it had been loyal to him until the middle of 2013. Its conquest was as significant as much as it was impenetrable because history reveals how, in that world, local interests still predominate, tribes choose this or that ally for their own advantage, and they weave and unmake alliances according to codes of honor and historical references that can be traced back through the centuries to the Prophet Mohammad.

Our reality is a thousand miles away from that logic, which instead explains how ISIS could become the master of all that territory and invent for itself a capital, Raqqa specifically. The city lies nearly 500 kilometers from Damascus, a distance that makes it almost impossible to maintain control of communications and supplies. Before the Syrian uprising, it was ruled by the Sharabeen tribe—a very simple and stubborn people, shepherds and cattle ranchers. To guarantee their loyalty and oppose the powerful, rich, and numerous tribes of the Shammar, who were leaning toward Saudi Arabia (where many of its members took refuge at the time), Bashar Assad's father Hafez resupplied the Sharabeen with weapons and money. In 2011, however, anti-government rebels had not only disarmed the Sharabeen but also put them on the run, which consequently brought back the pro-Saudi Shammar. This has caused great worry among all of the other fourteen local tribes, who turned to ISIS and requested protection. Here's how Raqqa passed peacefully and almost without a fight from the hands of Assad to ISIS, which has made it their capital.

Therefore, Raqqa has become a landmark case, a model city, fanatically jihadist, in which the severed heads of sinners are impaled on fences along the streets, women are black ghosts, and the guardians of the faith terrorize anyone who wants to just smoke a cigarette. However, people smile for the cameras, while adorable kids, well indoctrinated, explain that their dream is to kill a Westerner, a *kafir*, an infidel, by cutting off his head. Laughing, shouting "Takbir!" followed by the customary "Allah-u Akbar," they are ready to kill.

We have some difficulty thinking in terms of tribes, but it is precisely their existence that allowed ISIS's rapid consolidation. In Iraq, the prime minister imposed by the Americans, Nuri al-Maliki, a Shiite and friend of the Iranians, immediately found a way to alienate even those Sunni clans who had supported the American intervention. Al-Maliki acted as a bully and a fool, and tribes rebelled. Among them is one of the largest clans, the Dulaim, which occupies the richest area in terms of oil wells, the Anbar province. Demonstrations and clashes multiplied in an Iraq left imprudently to its own devices by the Americans, who were still providing aid to a prime minister hated by the people and supported by Iran. That's how, taking advantage of widespread Iraqi discontent, the most aggressive and belligerent fringe of Sunni rebels, Al-Qaeda, transformed into ISIS.

It is true that, as often happened in the Middle Ages, great leaders, for example the Dulaim, do not promise allegiance to anyone, not even today to al-Baghdadi; however, there is certainly room for fear, admiration, hope of acquiring power, and also excitement in seeing an old tribal code of four thousand years come back to life. In short, ISIS, under the bewildered eyes of Obama and Europe, has conquered territory, taken over large cities, and crossed and erased the borders with Syria, where—needless to say—the ensuing chaos from the revolt against Assad and the dictator's madly repressive clampdown had created an ideal breeding ground.

In a nutshell, two circumstances offered ISIS the necessary space to consolidate itself: the failure of the American reconstruction plan in Iraq and the anti-Assad revolt. The anger against a dull and bloodthirsty tyrant like Assad, as well as the horror of a war that caused 250,000 deaths and did not leave one stone unturned, has produced in Syrian rebels the desire to affiliate themselves with someone who would rescue them from the condition of stray dogs without a collar, bombed, hungry refugees unheard by Europe. ISIS said: "Here I am, I will show you the way, I am the truth, your general, your father and your mother."

## The Caliphate's Expansionist Aims

Syria and Iraq: these two unfortunate countries are the cradles of ISIS, but even more so is the Quran. Yes, because those who keep repeating that this phenomenon is not Islamic, that cruci-fixions have nothing to do with Islam, only harbor pious hopes. Instead, these things are relevant, as long as you decide to use a two-thousand-year-old text as a guide. They, ISIS's men, have made up their mind, no matter what any enlightened moder-ate Islamist may think. They are not modern; on the contrary they despise modernity. They are ancients and they value that, and if we let them do it they will drag us into a movie where the time machine is running backwards and we will be their vic-tims in the next scene, the one in which Jews and Christians are subjected, converted, or killed. The choice is ours. Others, apostates, atheists, Buddhists, Yazidis, Baha'is, all sentenced to death: they are not even in the ranks of *dhimmis*, non-Muslims residing in a region ruled by Sharia, but who believe in one God alone (which saves their lives), albeit with some unforgiv-able weirdness that relegates them to be, in an Islamic state, the last, reviled, mocked and without rights.

It was al-Zawahiri, in the company of the religious Jorda-nian Abu Muhammad al-Maqdisi, who began working hard on Salafi theories (from *Salaf al-salihin*, "the pious ancestors"), maintaining in the end that true Muslims cannot limit them-selves to contemporary practices. Indeed, one must criticize them and go back, back, and back again, following the models so clearly bequeathed from the seventh century, when Muham-mad explained his doctrine.

We have to be very clear, when we talk about ISIS, that this choice is explicit, that there is nothing crazy in its behavior, as one would come to think by observing it. Its momentary de-feats—which we witness while rejoicing, as if they were signs of a cinematic destiny in which the good guys always win—are part of a grand design written in history according to Allah's plan. As Jessica Lewis McFate and Harleen Gambhir wrote in the *Wall Street Journal*, "It is pursuing a deliberate strategy to offset its tactical losses in Iraq and Syria with territorial gains in the Mideast and globally."

Its goal, as the two authors maintain, is "to consolidate and expand itself": its complex global strategy has three geographical rings. The first ring is already won, including Iraq and *al-Sham*, namely, the Levantine State of Syria, Jordan, Lebanon, and the difficult but tasty morsel Palestine-Israel. Next comes the second ring, that of the surrounding area, which includes the rest of the Middle East and North Africa, in addition to Afghanistan and Pakistan to the east, bordering with the enemy Iran, territories where ISIS will bring their "governorships" to life. Then will come the third ring, the outermost one: the rest of the world, i.e., Europe, the United States, and Asia. Here, the Islamic State is mainly focused on Europe, which always names "Rome," referring not so much to modern Catholicism as the Byzantine Empire, the great and powerful adversary that started to decline during the birth of the first Islamic caliphate.

ISIS distinguishes between fully Islamic countries and countries hosting Muslim communities, and in each ring uses different but intertwined strategies, which seek to expand its influence. In the first ring, the caliphate, which lost Kobanî thanks to the determination of the Kurds and the U.S. drone air strikes, is holding ground in Raqqa, Deir al-Zor, Falzone Luja, and Mosul (cities with more than one million inhabitants) and in large areas of the Anbar province. The consolidation of areas already conquered in the first ring helps extend its reach to the weak states of the second, now ready to be conquered by the strongest, like Libya and Yemen, and of regions where militants can count on the ideological proximity to local clans, such as the Egyptian Sinai and parts of Saudi Arabia, Algeria, and, beyond, of Khorasan, the historical name of the region that includes parts of Iran, Pakistan, Afghanistan, and India.

ISIS often helps local clans to arm themselves and to carry out separate military actions, especially in Libya and in the Sinai. In this way, they form a number of satellite groups, such as the Islamic Youth Sura Council in Libya or the Ansar Beit al-Maqdis in the Sinai, hence preparing the ground for the future expansion of the Islamic State. Then it will be our turn.

## ISIS's War against the West

ISIS's current technique is to extend its influence in the West through terrorist and cyber attacks. According to the above-mentioned article, since the beginning of January 2015, groups of pro-ISIS hackers have stepped up their activities: for example, more than 19,000 cyber attacks targeted French websites in the week after the massacre at the satirical magazine *Charlie Hebdo* in Paris on January 7, 2015.

The effort in the third ring, the West, is mainly aimed at recruiting. ISIS recruits so-called "foreign fighters" through social networks, where young militants post videos in which they promise their peers a life full of meaning and with an important mission: to fight for Allah. Sacred music rendered through more modern tunes, sublime voices without the accompaniment of musical instruments, considered terrible diabolical contraptions to be banned for eternity by ISIS, combine with the text messages of recruiters—converted children of immigrants—that, in various languages, reach mobile phones and computers of Swedish, Irish, Dutch, and even Italian teenagers. They promise a new life, purified of the corruption of the West. They try to persuade them that the reason why they have no place in society is because of a culture that does not know how to appreciate them, while in ISIS's Islam they will be completely content.

The videos portray welcoming homes and lovely Western landscapes as horrible falsehoods, an alien invention of a reality that the recipients of the message will never be able to acquire, while the recruiter sits with his rifle in his hand in the shade of a tree and talks about his life now that he has found a reason for living. Then, after a few words of hatred toward infidels, he invites the young Westerners to join ISIS's ranks, instilling a sense of confidence and superiority, which attracts many outcasts. Sometimes the recruited are encouraged to stay in their countries of origin, becoming themselves recruiters and implementing attacks that are designed to polarize the attention of Western societies, directing it onto themselves and thereby avoiding attacks in Iraq and Syria. Later, at the right time, they will think about total war.

In short, the Islamic State is not just a vague entity down there, to the left on the map. What it has organized and is attempting to consolidate is a global network, capable of supporting a global terrorist campaign even if it loses terrain at home. It is a shield of defense even before the attack because without the black flag with its central, white *shahada*—the Islamic profession of faith ("There is no God but Allah, and Muhammad is his prophet")—the caliphate would be an empty and meaningless endeavor. Meanwhile, ISIS's flag flutters over a vast territory that designates the land that Muhammad wanted in the seventh century more than anything else, that is, the land of Islam. Therefore, ISIS battles first and foremost for land, but the metastases of that cancer are functional to the survival of its head.

While the Islamic State has declared open war on the West and is concerned about creating cells of loyal fighters in European cities, there is another Islamic danger. It has the same hatred while pursuing the same aims of conquest. It also professes the same contempt for Western civilization, even with the same violence, but presents itself as more friendly, willing, and open to dialogue. We must now speak of Iran in order to understand that the smiles of its politicians with trimmed beards and elegant clothes are not a sign of openness but a fraudulent way to deceive us and, finally, to acquire the atomic bomb to destroy us.

# CHAPTER 3

# The Shiite Revival

IN OUR IMAGINATION, therefore, there is this blaring danger, almost fantastical but very real, called ISIS. It terrorizes, it has a definite plan of action, and it has a solid doctrine that determines its every move. We will come back to address its aims and life models later.

But before we get back to discussing Syria and Iraq, places where the turbaned devil thrives and death's horsemen ride about on Humvees, we should reflect on a world that loves to show itself with two opposing faces, one in a jacket and white shirt, the other in the traditional imam's garb with beards of all kinds, white, black, pointy, round, but always combed and always at the ready to hand out sentences.

## The Islamic "Reconquest"

It may seem surprising that, during a possibly important negotiation occurring in March 2015, Iran's Supreme Leader, Ayatollah Seyyed Ali Hoseyni Khamenei, found it quite natural that the crowd which had gathered to hear him speak repeatedly shouted "Death to America!" in response, even while John Kerry, the American secretary of state, was shaking hands with Khamenei's minister, Mohammad Zarif.

In the shadows, militiamen, warriors, terrorists, and even armies at the service of the ayatollah's Iran work on this massive undertaking: the great comeback of the Shiite world, a world accounting for only 20 percent of Islam but heir to the Persian Empire, and to its cruelty as much as its grace.

In more recent times, newspapers have been filled with general approval for the agreement that U.S. President Obama closed with Khamenei's Iran in order to delay—yes, delay, for a mere decade, not put an end to—the pro-Iranian nuclear program, a program that soon will be able to produce an atomic bomb. This is an even more pressing issue than the Sunni terror that we've been describing up to now. Or rather, let's put it this way, a matter just as serious. We'll come back to this in a bit. It is, however, fundamental to understand that Iran is the second vise-clamp that wants to crush the West. Whoever thinks this is an exaggerated reading doesn't understand Islamism.

First and foremost Islam as a whole, both Sunni and Shia, believes that the preceding religions, Judaism and Christianity, have been led astray and followed false doctrines, and they have been replaced by God's perfect and definitive revelation, conveyed through the Quran. This is why they call the pre-Islamic era *jahiliyya*, "the age of ignorance." In short, before Islam, there's a great historical darkness of which nothing is of value or interest and whose vestiges must be forgotten or, worse, destroyed. It was no random act when the Taliban in Afghanistan demolished the two famous Buddhas of Bamiyan, carved in the first century B.C., two colossal statues, 53 and 38 meters high, carved into the face of the mountains in the Bamiyan Valley, a province about 230 kilometers from Kabul. The Silk Road once passed through this area; who can say how many merchants and travelers saw these statues and spoke of them. However, since they were not Islamic and considered idols of the infidels, Mullah Omar, the Taliban's leader, ordered them destroyed in

March 2001. After explosives and cannon fire reduced them to dust, the Taliban immediately celebrated "the destruction of the idols."

ISIS does this as well. In February 2015, its men merrily went to work demolishing precious artifacts inside the Mosul Museum: statues and bas-reliefs of the ancient civilization of Mesopotamia, where the very idea of a code of laws first took hold, where the written word was born, as well as the first forms of organized city-states, both independent and federated, from which the first empires that dominated the Middle East were created. Now, with craven zeal, these men forced an entry into the municipal museum, threw statues to the ground, and smashed them with sledgehammers. Their imperative is to erase anything that existed before Islam and anything that does not represent Islam, both perceived as a perennial threat.

The desire to dominate is common among many civilizations. Even Christians built churches where pagan temples and synagogues once stood. Likewise, to this day Islam continues to do that which it has always done: leave its mark wherever it goes in order to prove that it is the sole possessor of the one true faith. The Quranic inscriptions in the Dome of the Rock in Jerusalem, also known as the Mosque of Omar, testify to this practice. Completed in 691 over the razed clearing where the ancient Temple of Solomon (the Beit ha-Miqdash) once stood, this mosque, together with the Al-Aqsa Mosque, occupies the space that was once the center of Jewish life. In this same vein, the inscription appearing on the dinar, the first currency minted by the Umayyad caliphs at the end of the seventh century, reads: "Your faith is corrupted, your time is past, I am now the ruler of God's empire on earth." From Medina, Damascus, Baghdad, Cairo, and from Istanbul up to Constantinople and Vienna, the battle was waged under this insignia, and the aspiration to annihilate other civilizations in order to satisfy God's will has always been part of jihad's vigorous and violent doctrine.

Even today there is no shortage of analogous occurrences, such as the banner that Christian pilgrims visiting the Holy Sepulcher are forced to read at the entrance of the nearby Mosque of Omar, which Saladin rebuilt in 1187 after having negotiated a new conquest of the city: "Jesus said that the true religion is Islam." Or consider the violent controversy over Nazareth, where Muslims want to build a new mosque right next to the Basilica of the Annunciation. It seems that at least for now the project has been put on hold. The history of Islam is full of similar signs of domination.

Many truces have been made with infidel enemies, following in the Prophet's footsteps, but these truces (*hudna*) and Islam's famous tolerance were always born on a conditional and temporary basis, subject to annulment when faced with situations deemed not useful to, or harmful to, Islam. Through the centuries, this religion has always seen itself as engaged in a holy war, persecuted by adverse powers, and always in a position of either victory or defeat, never peace. The very idea of a treaty with a non-Muslim power, or of a contract with an infidel, is foreign to Islam, whose philosophical history considers the world a huge battlefield where Allah's faithful must fight the infidels with whom, naturally, there can merely be truces, but never lasting peace.

Therefore, the Quran warns Muslims, in Sura 5: "O you who believe! Do not take the Jews and the Nazarenes for friends; they are friends of each other; and whoever amongst you takes them for a friend, then surely he is one of them; surely Allah does not guide the unjust people" (verse 51). Further on we read: "You will see many of them befriending those who disbelieve; certainly evil is that which their souls have sent before for them, that Allah became displeased with them and in chastisement shall they abide" (verse 80).

Islam considers the contemporary age and its relations with the infidel West in the same manner. After the fall of the Ottoman Empire, the colonial powers created new states in the former Ottoman territories, believing that they could give rise to societies formed in accordance with European models, that is to say, Arab democracies, particularly in Lebanon, a Christian enclave in the Muslim world. Democracy, however, has not taken root there, because it is considered a wicked, alien imposition from the West.

Since then, pan-Islamist movements have been fighting to eliminate Western influences and to return to the old Islam. The incessant friction with Europe's colonial nations is still very present. Although Europeans remained in the Middle East for less than a hundred years, and though their presence there never so much as approached the levels of colonialism carried out in Africa or the Far East, the Islamic world nonetheless translates anti-colonialist rhetoric into anti-Western hatred.

This hatred for the West did not prevent them, however, from importing at least one European ideology, which would be embraced with zeal: Nazism. By the end of the 1930s, there were Nazi parties and youth organizations in the Arab states and copies of *Mein Kampf* in circulation, spreading its supremacist ideology and hatred for the Jews who were building the new state of Israel in their ancestral land.

The Arab alliance with Hitler's Germany was an attempt on the part of the Arabs to ally with a power that offered weapons against the new presence of Israel and European imperialism in the Middle East. The Grand Mufti of Jerusalem, Haj Amin al-Husseini, expelled by the British, took refuge in Berlin after a brief stop in Rome and aided his ally, Hitler, by creating a group of militants comprised entirely of Muslim neo-Nazis, the Hanjar troops, in Bosnia. Even today, *Mein Kampf* is a welcome read among the Arab public and can be found in any bookshop, from Ramallah to the United Arab Emirates.

After the fall of Nazi Germany, the Arab world, which still opposed the idea of liberal democracy, sought the support of the Soviet Union against the United States. Later, with the support of Osama bin Laden—who was already laying the foundation for a nascent Al-Qaeda—the Taliban waged war against the Soviet occupation in Afghanistan, convincing Islamists that the Taliban was the victorious force through which they could once again aspire to world domination. Just as Islam had defeated the Soviet Union (this being the conclusion that Al-Qaeda and Taliban leaders had reached at that time), so too would it easily defeat the United States, the Western enemy *par excellence*, the other hated, unholy, and aggressive superpower considered the cause of Islam's present state of ruin.

Al-Qaeda's strategy was born out of this idea. In 2001, in the hopes of bringing about a total American defeat, Al-Qaeda planned and executed the attack on the Twin Towers, an event that, we must admit, has effectively changed the world, as well as U.S. policy. In observing these events, we must understand once and for all that Islam can truly devastate Western civilization—even if its tactics differ from conventional military conquest—and that its threats are by no means simply rhetoric or a bluff.

Islam always speaks clearly, for that we have to give it credit: Osama's threats were blunt and precise. When he declared war against the "Crusaders" and against the Jews, he knew exactly what he was saying; and when Khomeini, exiled in France, promised the establishment of an Islamist regime in which Sharia would dominate and which would strive for world domination, he was detailed in his intentions. Middle East scholars, not knowing Farsi, could not read his pronouncements, but

Professor Bernard Lewis could and was thus able to warn the world of what was about to happen. It was the same thing Lewis did in the years when bin Laden was publicizing his proclamations. However, people judged him a patsy, together with us, his devoted students.

We have seen in the preceding chapters what ISIS wants and how this new organization that threatens our civilization functions. We will also see that there are certain paths we can take in constructing a rational counteroffensive to defeat this mindless zombie-like aggression.

## The Shiite Grip

First of all, we must understand where this coalition lies. In reality, it covers a vast and jagged area. In short, we can say that there are two Islamic forces that, like a nutcracker, are trying to grab our head and crush it (it almost seems like a scene from a movie to me, with the sweet, blond, smiling Federica Mogherini, EU High Representative for Foreign Affairs, reaching out to Mohammad Zarif to seal the deal, he with this satisfied look on his face, looking her up and down like a courtly wolf and thinking, "The better to eat you, my child!"). They intend to bring about our elimination. Actually, no, first they want our submission.

The Sunni faction, the majority within the Islamic world (making up about 80 percent of Muslims), is rich and powerful thanks to oil, and is responsible for the creation of ISIS along with Al-Qaeda, the Taliban, Jabhat al-Nusra, Hamas, Boko Haram…among many other organizations (above all the Muslim Brotherhood, a disguise for destructive Islamic extremism). It's a big world divided into many realities. Shiites, on the other hand, who also avail themselves of various militias (Hezbollah, Houthi, etc.) with quite a few sub-branches, are aware of their minority status in the Muslim world and demand compensation for having been victims of an older brother who judges them with obvious contempt, and very often regards them as mortal enemies.

Let us consider how ISIS members attack their Shiite brethren today with cannibalistic cruelty. The first thing they do when they occupy a village or a building is to ask who among the inhabitants is Shiite. They will be killed first, while those who claim to be Sunni are required to prove it in the form of names, addresses, tokens, or the recitation of prayers. After this mock trial, if they are unable to convince their attackers, victims often suffer the horrible fate of the idolaters and corrupters of their religion: terrified, kneeling, asking pardon, and swearing allegiance to the enemy, only to be beheaded or shot in the neck.

Shiites have suffered greatly at the hands of their fellow believers in Allah and the prophet Muhammad, and sometimes you have to wonder how a doctrinal difference as small as the one that distinguishes them from Sunnis could be the cause of the worst of all the world's current bloodshed. The difference is this: the Prophet died in 632, and his companions chose Abu Bakr as his successor, who became the first caliph. He did not possess any fundamental religious role, but he was entrusted with the duty of ensuring the continuity of the victorious march of the Prophet on the surrounding territories and beyond. In short, it was a political and military role; the leader was a warrior who was to clear the way for conquering the world in the light of the Prophet's precepts.

The opposing party on the other hand, namely, the Shiites, believed that Muhammad's son-in-law, Ali, should become not only the new leader but also the spiritual guide who would lead Islam to world domination through a violent revival. In the year 680 at Karbala, in present-day Iraq, a coalition of Umayyads and Yazidis defeated the troops of Hussein, Ali's second son.

Islam was split between the followers of the caliphs and the followers of the "house of Ali," *shiat 'Ali*, that is, the Shiites. Hussein is considered history's first martyr, with martyrdom occupying a central place in Shiite theological doctrine. Ali's followers were persecuted, expelled from Arab territories, and eventually resettled in the Persian Empire, which converted to Shiism at the beginning of the sixteenth century. Shiites have continued for centuries to visit Karbala in pilgrimage, increasing their outrage and their thirst for revenge against the Sunni usurpers.

The majority of Shiites belong to the branch of the Twelvers, so named because they believe in the sequence of twelve successive Imams to Muhammad. According to the Shiites, after the schism, the Twelfth Imam, Muhammad ibn Hassan al-Mahdi, a direct descendent of Ali born in 869, suddenly and mysteriously disappeared at age 72 to escape his enemies. In his "divine concealment" he prepares his return and the coming of the Day of Judgment. In every age, the Mahdi's return has always been announced as near. Today, it is considered imminent. This doesn't bode well for us.

Although the theological differences are minimal, Shiites have developed different practices and different interpretations of the sacred texts, which in the eyes of the Sunnis are heresy punishable by death. Furthermore, they consider imams, their religious leaders, as men inspired by God. Their cry for revenge, however, has been silenced, and over the centuries they have developed the concept of *taqiyya* (translated as *idtirar* for the Sunni world), or dissimulation, which allows a believer to violate Islamic precepts and, in essence, to lie for the sake of his or her life or for the greater good of the community, an attitude that recalls the policy of Iranian leaders today...

Marginalized as a persecuted minority—those who believe themselves to be the true heirs of Muhammad—the Shiites have always nurtured the doctrine of jihad. Historical conditions, though, kept religious leaders away from politics, giving them solely the role of spiritual leaders and jurisconsult for the political leadership. Khomeini changed all of this and brought political power into the hands of the ayatollahs, the religious guides, thus upsetting the whole of Islam and guaranteeing vengeance for the Shiites against the entire Muslim world. This vengeance is destined to overturn the same Sunni supremacy that had persecuted and humiliated Shiites everywhere, a supremacy to which the Shiites aspire in the struggle for the leadership of Islam.

## The Return of the Mahdi

Waiting for the return of the Mahdi has helped the Shiites survive the awful suffering and oppression inflicted on them by the Sunni majority, which has always considered the Shiites traitors of the Quran and idolaters of their Imam. Hope in the coming Mahdi has inspired them directly in their policy choices since 1979, when the Islamic Revolution took the upper hand in Iran and Khomeini described himself as the Mahdi's representative in Allah's first government in the world. It also helped them organize themselves and stay united, sometimes with great success. This is also a pattern that reemerges over time: the same thing happened, for example, with the seizure of power of the Safavid dynasty in Persia in 1500, thanks to which that ancient nation, now Iran, became forever the Shiite country *par excellence.*

Shiites know that all of their suffering will come to an end, along with all the injustices that weigh on the world, when the Mahdi comes. The signs say that we should get ready, that his coming is at hand. The two figures destined to lead the preparation of the advent of the Mahdi, Ayatollah Khamenei and Hassan Nasrallah (the leader of the Lebanese Shiite group

Hezbollah), explain it in detail. The Mahdi will appear, Ahmadinejad has said repeatedly, "When the world has fallen into chaos, and war rages between the races, without reason." That is, in order to ensure the reappearance of the Mahdi, there must be a worldwide conflagration. Scholars explain with clarity that the Islamic Republic seeks with determination to create an explosive situation. It's not at all concerned, as we would be, about a possible war, much less a nuclear war, but rather is only interested in creating the conditions for the advent of the Mahdi. Actually, it will go to any length to create those conditions. Not all of the Iranian leadership may believe in it, but the influence of Mahdism is great.

Ahmadinejad's presidency represented the most extreme expression of the Islamic Republic's messianic attitude. He had, in fact, used Mahdism as a means to create publicity for himself: railing against the Iranian political establishment, whose corruption and submissiveness would prolong the wait for the messianic coming, he managed to make his way up to the municipal government of Tehran, and later to the country's presidency. Messianism has therefore been integral to his politics. In 2005, he sponsored the first international conference on Mahdism, defining this ideology as essential for the survival of humanity and for peace among religions. His advisors were then worried about rendering the ideology more sophisticated, quoting and reinterpreting Heidegger and his critique of rational thought, and reinforcing anti-Americanism and anti-Semitism. Also, speaking from the UN podium on September 26, 2012, after the customary insults against Israel and the United States, Ahmadinejad promised a new global government established by the Mahdi and his servant Jesus, whose coming would be imminent.

However, if you do some digging, it turns out that even the more credible figures today (credible because they are seen as moderate), such as President Hassan Rouhani, show unmistakable signs of Mahdism. When he was elected in 2013, Rouhani immediately declared, "This political choice is thanks to the gentle grace of the last Islamic messiah," that is, the Mahdi. Additionally, the powerful ayatollah Aydallah Moyahedi Kemani, Tehran's official preacher for Friday prayers, has stated, "Before the reappearance of Imam Zaman [the Mahdi] the battle will peak, there will be no mercy even for the mother's womb."

A part of Iran's nomenklatura, including two foreign ministers, belonged to a secret society, later abolished, that was working to promote the advent of the Mahdi, and actually challenged the Khomeini doctrine, the *velayat-e faqih*, the "Rule of the Jurisprudent." The latter guaranteed temporal power to the country's clerics and effectively made them Iran's true political leaders, an authentic revolution in the Shiite world. But for those belonging to this secret society, the Mahdi would soon assume all power directly. One of the most prominent figures is, of course, the commander of the Revolutionary Guards, Brigadier General Mohammad Ali Jafari, who in 2008 in a speech delivered to a group of officers, stated, "Our Imam did not limit the movement of the Islamic Revolution to this country, but drew greater horizons. Our duty is to prepare the way for an Islamic world government and the rule of the Lord of the Time [the Mahdi]."

The atomic bomb, the destruction of Israel, the breaking of nuclear pacts all figure perfectly in this plan—they stem from this plan actually—a plan that has been repeatedly confirmed and reiterated by the highest echelons of power in Iran. Many typical behaviors of Iran's leadership can't be explained without making reference to the messianic inspirations that determine them: this applies to the obsessive repetition of hatred and violence against the United States, Israel, the West, traitors of Islam, or against this or that and so on. It applies as well to the great lengths Iran goes to to sink money into sophisticated weaponry, first-class ballistic warheads, tens of thousands of missiles in the hands of Hezbollah, terrorist attacks financed throughout the world, the maintenance of the *Basij* militia and all the other savage militias, all trained and ready with a suitcase full of bullets to go and wage war in Iraq, Yemen, Lebanon… (I'll point out that Iran's funds have dwindled quite a lot due to the sanctions leveled against it because of its unchecked atomic enrichment program, a program that they will now be able to increase exponentially after the agreement with the P5+1.)

## Iranian Imperialism

In 1979, when the revolution that overthrew the Shah broke out in Iran, this great uprising was completely misunderstood by our naïve souls. Journalists who followed the event made it out to be a popular revolution of the poor against the rich, of self-determination against an oppressive, imperial domination supported by the Americans, with Shah Reza Pahlavi (wrongfully) depicted as a cruel puppet dressed in white and gold, an enemy of the people, whom he starved and locked away in prisons, while Khomeini was portrayed as an old wise sage who cared deeply about the fate of his people.

The Shah had in fact implemented an unfortunate series of flip-flops between Westernization and repression until, in 1978, he had gone too far, carrying out a full-blown massacre in Piazza Jaleh, an event that would cost him the throne a year later. Still, the government of the ayatollahs has far surpassed the Shah in cruelty toward their internal enemies, who today are probably to be found in even greater numbers, though they are forced into silence. The Khomeinist revolution, however, had seduced many intellectuals, including Michel Foucault, in the recalcitrant search for an alternative to liberal democracy.

As soon as he became Supreme Leader, Khomeini immediately gave several signs that the new regime's arrogance was worse than that of the previous one. The ayatollahs were not messing around: women who dared to dress in Western-style clothing were given lashes (there was a famous case of an unfortunate woman who was discovered wearing lipstick; she was sentenced to 101 lashes). Fury swept over the youth of the nation to such an extent that universities were evacuated and closed when students showed any signs of political or intellectual activity. Every day a new law, a new Islamic ruling made Iran hell for Christians, Jews, women, and homosexuals, which I'll come back to in a little bit.

On the international stage, the occupation of the U.S. Embassy in Tehran in 1979 gave a clear signal of the new regime's unusual aggressiveness toward an America that stood by flummoxed and powerless. On November 4 of that same year, a group of Islamist students stormed the U.S. Embassy and took staff and marine security guards hostage. A few embassy employees managed, however, to take refuge in other embassies and would later be taken out of the country disguised as Canadian television crewmembers thanks to a secret service operation. The remaining 52 captives were freed after 444 days. At the time, Khomeini applauded the initiative of these students who were galvanized by his words of hatred against America, which the ayatollah called the "Great Satan." Even at that time, however, America already proved itself loath in its political relations with the new Middle East.

Then there's the Khomeini doctrine of exporting the revolution that Iran set in motion, first with attacks in the Gulf, followed by the war against Iraq, and finally with the establishment of terrorist cells first in Lebanon, with Hezbollah, and later, even among Sunnis who answer to him, with Hamas among the Palestinians, and now with the Houthi in Yemen.

Awaiting the Mahdi had its great moment of glory during Ahmadinejad's presidency, but the fact is that it remains a very influential part of the Shiite experience, and the Iranian ruling class bears signs of this, just like a Christian who believes in the Gospel's message of the salvation of the world, or a religious Jew in the coming of a Messiah who will finally establish an era of justice. Unfortunately, however, the Mahdi comes with violence, destruction, and chaos: both in their scriptures and in the popular sentiment, there is a push toward preparing for war, both at home and abroad. They aren't just going to sit around waiting for the Mahdi to come!

We have explained how the warring Sunnis are going to great lengths to achieve a universal caliphate, but the warring Shiites are doing their part as well. Their plan of action is aimed well beyond solely the establishment of a caliphate, and extends to the fulfillment of the coming apocalypse.

Iran is very specific about this. A text used by the Mahdists states the following: "Ali's prize will come from Yemen and Iraq." It's not by chance that the Shia today are basically creating new Islamic States to their liking, that is, Islamic states intended to contribute to the much-awaited apocalypse, obviously via an imperialistic Iranian supremacy that has already been outlined: Iraq is effectively controlled by Iran since its Shiite leadership couldn't do without the military support of the Shiite General Qassam Soleimani, the high-ranking official responsible for Iranian foreign operations, a skilled and omnipresent wildcard; Syria's Assad, who belongs to the Alawites, a sect close to the Shiites, would not be able to survive without the fierce supplementary assistance of Hezbollah, which is financed by Iran, or without help from the Islamic Revolutionary Guard Corps (IRGC), which has allowed him to stay in power despite a revolt that has lasted for five years and the appalling massacres he has orchestrated against his own people.

In Lebanon, where the individual religious components are so varied as to make this the only pluralist state in the Middle East, Hezbollah terrorizes the country and crushes it under the Shiite heel.

Further south on the map, where power means controlling the Bab al-Mandab Strait, which handles 40 percent of maritime traffic and controls the Suez Canal, Yemen too falls prey to the craven appetite of the ayatollah's imperialism, their central government coming under attack by Houthi militias. Therefore, even Sana'a, like Baghdad, Damascus, Beirut, and Tehran of course, is part of the Iranian empire's project, the project of a great territorial power, head to head against Sunni forces. Just as the Sunnis of ISIS seek to destroy the Shia in order to expand the caliphate, the Shiites attempt to deal with the Sunnis in the same manner.

Just to prove that the Shiites won't lend a hand to the West to combat ISIS out of a mere sense of goodwill, take a look at Iranian society; it looks just like the one established by ISIS, even if its style is a little more subdued. They have good public relations, and the country can vaunt the objective charm of ancient Persian civilization and eighteenth-century-style manners.

## Living in Tehran

Living in Tehran is unsettling, often dangerous, and sometimes lethal. The regime is felt everywhere. The streets are still patrolled by morality police, who stop girls that don't wear a cloak covering at least until their knees or whose veil does not quite cover enough of their foreheads. They also stop boys if their clothing style is too Western, if they wear torn pants or earrings or have long hair. Nonsense? Not really! Sometimes for the "appalling indecency" of a strand of hair escaping from under the veil they end up at the central police station to be whipped. Not to mention a couple in love who wants to take a walk or have a coffee together—forbidden! A woman, in order to travel, still needs to have her guardian's permission, i.e., a husband or a male relative. To enter many public offices the veil is not enough; it also takes the *chador*, that is, the black sheet that completely obscures a woman's body.

The regime of the ayatollahs is very careful to avoid too much publicity, but according to reports by journalists and associations for human rights, they are still carrying out death sentences by stoning for adultery. The last execution took place in 2011. Iran's parliament tried to eliminate this sentence from the penal code in 2012, but the ayatollah's Supreme Council promptly reintroduced it in 2013.

There are other "appalling" crimes such as sodomy. In a speech given at Columbia University in September 24, 2007, Ahmadinejad declared that homosexuals don't exist in Iran, to which the public retorted sarcastically that Iran must have already exterminated them all. Ahmadinejad's statement was perhaps not entirely false because gays in Iran are either hanged or forced to change their sex. The ayatollahs say gender reassignment is not against the Quran. Therefore, the official policy of the regime encourages homosexuals to do it. Those who can do so flee to Turkey and then, through the UN High Commissioner for Refugees (UNHCR), carry on to make a life for themselves in a country that accepts them, even though it is becoming increasingly difficult to be considered for refugee status based on sexual identity in many European countries. Those who remain must resign themselves to a sex change if they don't want to run the risk of a certain death, dangling from a gallows in a public square.

Iranians don't like their regime. In 2009, when it was discovered that Ahmadinejad's second election was rigged, they weren't afraid to face torture and a bloodbath in order to try overthrowing the regime. Today, in fact, many Iranians still dream of a coup. The regime's endeavor to make its repression seem a little less brutal lies in making those punishments that are directly inspired by Sharia law, such as stoning, cutting off hands, or the physical elimination of homosexuals, rare, without altogether eliminating them. Nonetheless, it's the laws of the country that determine its orientation as an extreme Islamist state, so extreme in fact that from the summer of 2013, when Rouhani was elected, through to the first year of his mandate, there were 773 executions, in contrast to 530, which occurred during Mahmoud Ahmadinejad's last year in office. On October 25, 2015, the 26-year-old Reyhaneh Jabbari was hanged after having been found guilty of killing the former intelligence officer Morteza Abdolali Sarbandi, who had tried to rape her. Before being killed, Reyhaneh was held in isolation and tortured. Women enjoy special treatment when they are in prison, especially when they're sentenced to death. Prison guards often rape them as a good deed, not wanting—should these women be virgins—their impure souls to make it to paradise, where only the purest of souls may reside.

In all civil and criminal transactions a woman's testimony is worth only half that of a man's. In order for her testimony to be equal to a man's, either two women are needed or the presence of a man is required. Everyone cites the fact that there are more women than men enrolled at university. This really isn't surprising, however, since university offers girls a way to delay marriage, which for women is legal at nine years old. Furthermore, it offers them a means to circumvent the fact that they are barred from many employment sectors.

Iranian law establishes the size of the stones to be used for stoning. They must be neither too large, so as not to kill right away, nor too small, so as to guarantee that every blow proves very painful. Bodily mutilations come in all forms, but human rights organizations have made lists of them so horrible that I prefer to spare the reader from their descriptions here. Many crimes are punished with a certain number of lashes delivered in a public square, much like what happens in territories occupied by ISIS. Music must be approved by the regime. The Internet is censored, and only certain sites can be accessed. Moreover, alcohol, fraternizing between young men and women, women's clothing, and the free exchange of opinions are—as Azar Nafisi's best-selling book *Reading Lolita in Tehran* details—all forbidden, and the morality police tirelessly patrol the streets, universities, and shops to ensure that their order is respected.

If you are Jew, Christian, Zoroastrian (Persia's ancient religion), or worse, a Baha'i, there's no helping you. The infidels do have their seat in parliament, because Islamic law happens to dictate this, but they should not even think of trying to make a career for themselves or of traveling freely abroad, or, in the case of Jews, of having contact with any relatives that might be in Israel. The Jews above all are held to be spies in the service of the Little Satan, Israel, a tradition started by Khomeini in 1979 with the hanging of Habib Elghanian. Everyone in Iran avoids speaking of the Jews in order not to annoy the regime. Of the Baha'i, the followers of a faith, born in nineteenth-century Persia, that fuses monotheistic religions with the Eastern traditions of Krishna and Buddha, not a word is spoken. They have no rights, as they are considered Islamic apostates (in that they recognize Muhammad), they can't have access to universities, their holy places are destroyed, and the newspapers call them "Zionist spies" because they have their headquarters in Haifa, where their founder, exiled from Persia, was buried.

Journalists are harassed on a daily basis, and media organizations that don't sing the regime's praises are subject to inspection and decimated by charges and detentions accompanied by torture. An entirely arbitrary order is enforced in the country, subservient to the great interests of billionaires and mafiosi who themselves answer to untouchable religious and political figures, the very same people funding terrorist militias abroad. Corruption is the most common topic of conversation among Iranians, such as how, in December 2004, after the famous earthquake that killed 70,000 people in the city of Bam, the tents donated by Germany were sold on the black market by the mullahs who were supposed to charitably distribute them among the evacuees. The drug market is rampant, connected to ruthless mafias that traffic drugs from Afghanistan, with Iran being one of their best clients.

## Iran's Expansionist Aspirations

Let us leave aside nuclear strategy for the moment—we will discuss it later—and address Iran's determination to "destroy that cancerous tumor," which is the way Iranian leaders continue to describe the State of Israel. Unfortunately these two goals are connected for one simple reason: it's not possible to believe how important it is for Iran to build an atomic bomb and destroy Israel if you don't understand that these two objectives have a religious basis, the very basis on which the Islamic Republic is founded. All of this is connected to their religious beliefs. As President Ahmadinejad has explained time and time again, even in his speech before the UN, the advent of the Mahdi is near and wars can help accelerate the arrival of that joyous day for humanity.

Ahmadinejad stated repeatedly, even on official occasions, his certainty that the Mahdi would probably appear during the course of his mandate. Happy to have shared his faith with the world ("I felt at once that the atmosphere had changed, for

27–28 minutes none of the [UN] delegates flinched") and having invested millions in the reconstruction of places holy to the Mahdi, Ahmadinejad, in a meeting with Philippe Douste-Blazy, the French minister of foreign affairs, asked, "Do you know why we should wish for chaos at any price?" before continuing, "Because after the chaos we will see the greatness of Allah." In other words, the more violent the clash, the nearer is the coming of the Mahdi.

Now, it's not that Shiites fully share Ahmadinejad's messianic enthusiasm, despite having elected him president twice, but messianism has certainly received a good push forward by the IRGC and other bellicose forces in the country since the war against Iraq in 1980. In the army, in fact, they used to lead an actor dressed in white on a white horse to the frontline, and he would bless the troops while they sang praises to the Mahdi look-alike.

Iranians are proud of their minority religion and of belonging to the great Persian civilization, which they consider worthily intertwined with Shia; even the quiet and elegant Foreign Minister Zarif, directly appointed by Khamenei, recently said "I don't understand Westerners, my culture is Shiite," while the P5+1 deluded themselves into believing they had established a closer relationship with him. Incidentally, he has referred to the American embassy in Tehran as "a nest of spies."

Since we have already talked about the cruelty of Sunni ISIS and its ideals and behaviors, it is natural to wonder what sort of life models this other Muslim face of the Islamic universe proposes.

Let's start from the war against Iraq in 1980, which was motivated by a fresh and virulent revolutionary zeal in Iran. Attempting to beat the Iraqi army, which was better equipped, the imams sent hordes of twelve- to fifteen-year-old boys into battle. With a plastic key produced in China around their necks—the key of paradise—they sent them forward in waves as they blew up into the air, clearing the field of mines in order to prepare the way for soldiers. Already in the first two years of the war, Iran had recovered all the territories it had lost to Saddam Hussein, but it preferred to continue the carnage for another six years. Clarifying his country's ambitious aims, in the meantime, Khomeini began to define himself as the "Supreme Leader of Muslims"—rather than solely of Iran—as the Sunni caliph does. This was actually a theological novelty, which he himself introduced, given that in classical Shiism imams should not play a political role, but solely a religious one.

Terrorism meanwhile quickly became a routine event. Terrorists with passports issued by the Iranian embassy perpetrated the attack on the Khobar Towers in Saudi Arabia. From the 1983 massacre of U.S. marines and French soldiers in Lebanon, to the attack on the Jewish community of Buenos Aires in 1994, to the more recent attack in 2012 on Israeli tourists in Burgas, Bulgaria, Hezbollah has been Tehran's preferred weapon, though many Iranian militant groups have been directly involved in these operations. Terrorism is the jihadist essence of Iranian Shiite ideology. For this reason, despite the historical differences and (albeit minimal) theological differences, Iran has sought allies in the Sunni world, such as Hamas in Gaza and Al-Qaeda in the 1990s, back when Hezbollah trained this rising star of international terrorism. Iran also maintains good relations with Sudan, where it manages military training camps.

Lately Iran has been trying to appear as open as possible. After all, it skillfully led a key negotiation to remedy its desperate economic conditions, which had become rather dire because of sanctions. In the end, it must also continue to fund its uranium enrichment program, despite the agreements of July 14, 2015, and, above all, its war machine, the militias it uses abroad, the *basij* who maintain order domestically, and the Al-Quds troops (*Al-Quds* being the Arabic name for Jerusalem) who respond solely to the Supreme Leader Khamenei and are used for the training of terrorist groups and for mysterious missions abroad.

But the time has come to discuss the real great danger that the West—rather than confronting and destroying it—has inaugurated with the Vienna Agreement: a nuclear Iran.

# CHAPTER 4

# Iran and the Bomb

THE PRE-ISLAMIC PERIOD, known as *jahiliyya*—the "age of ignorance"—is not a source of pride for the Arabs. However, the Iranians aren't Arabs; on the contrary, the Shiites have a discreet detachment from the Arab world, if not to say contempt. Arabs would be "camel milk drinkers and lizard eaters who dare aspire to the divine throne." Iranians remember well the role that the Persian Empire played in past eras: until very recently, the world called their great country "Persia" (80 million inhabitants), and their language, appearance, traditions, and historical memory all render them distinct members of the Islamic community.

Iran, at the time of the Safavids, had an imperial past that started in 1501 and lasted an impressive 220 years. Its founder, the Shah Ismail, established the Shia of the Twelfth Imam. The cult of martyrdom and the notion of *taqiyya* (dissimulation) went hand in hand with an incredible ability in diplomatic conduct; therefore Shah Abbas, in the seventh century, pretended to convert to Christianity in order to strengthen his alliance with the Portuguese, while he was negotiating with the British, who eventually helped him to expel the former from the Persian Gulf.

Iranians remember very well the borders of the Safavid empire, which reached up to Central Asia, with Iraq to the west, Afghanistan and Pakistan to the east, and the Persian Gulf in the south. So too do the Saudis, writes former Israeli ambassador to the UN and political analyst Dore Gold. Iranians told a high level U.S. official: "You have allowed the Persians, the Safavids, to take over Iraq." In short, Iran extends its tentacles with the conviction that it has every right to make the Middle East its base before taking over the world. The strategy to possess nuclear weapons in the Middle East is an absolute novelty, except with regard to Israel, which has built an indispensible defense shield in response, a blunt and simple declaration that tells everyone: "Never again" or "Noli me tangere" after the Shoah. Only ideological and partisan figures, like Günter Grass, God rest his soul, pretended to believe that an Israeli bomb was like a Chinese or Iranian bomb, built to attack.

No Middle Eastern country, albeit motivated by hegemonic ambitions such as Saudi Arabia or Egypt, has thought to implement a plan of total domination such as the one that would guarantee them nuclear capabilities.

## A Far-Reaching Strategy

In 1979, Khomeini established the Islamic Republic and with it a constitution that calls for the "continuation of the revolution at home and abroad." On Iran he said, "We do not worship Iran, we worship Allah. For patriotism is another name for paganism. I say let this land burn. I say let this land go up in smoke, provided Islam emerges triumphant in the rest of the world."

Clear, right? From its very inception, and even during the years of the war with Iraq, the Islamic Republic has never ceased showing its true face. Without ever disapproving them or openly claiming responsibility, it has made its continuous acts of terrorism, described in the previous chapter, its salient trait. Iran, for those who have not understood, has wanted (and wants) to show that through Hezbollah it can attack America, France, England, Germany, and the entire world, which needs to be converted. That is the purpose of terrorism: it doesn't only have the practical goal of frightening and bringing havoc, but it's also a flyer, a textbook, a nomination that is presented, just like ISIS does today with its severed heads.

From the Iranian strategy dictated by the Khomeinist doctrine, the thrust to extend the war to the world becomes apparent, passing (like ISIS) across the Middle East and, primarily, into the Shia–Sunni conflict with the 1980 war against Iraq (undertaken only twelve months after the revolution, and lasting for eight very bloody years).

Once, in Bethlehem, I happened to interview a terrorist on the run in the face of Israeli forces who wanted him. It was during the Second Intifada. The interview was conducted in a secret place, reached after many labyrinthine circles. The fugitive's bodyguards remained very nervously alert the entire time, and eventually, when they realized that I was Jewish, I only narrowly managed to get away. I tell this story because, among other things that the man revealed to me, the one that struck me in particular was his confession of having converted from Sunna to Shia Islam. This fact turned out to be so important that David Wurmser, Cheney's adviser on the Middle East, informed Cheney himself, who expressed his concern on the matter.

I realized later that many Palestinians, especially those hanging around Damascus, where Hamas had its headquarters, and who were the most determined to fight Israel to their death, had followed the road of indoctrination driven by their Syrian friends and by Hezbollah. This is why, despite its alliance with Iran, Hamas, in January 2012, severely hit the Shiite community in Gaza by closing down organizations that Hezbollah and

Iran were financing and assaulting converts who gathered near the Jabalia refugee camp to celebrate the end of *Arbain* (the forty days of mourning for Imam Hussein), in order to give a clear message of who is in charge in Gaza.

Not long ago I learned that in Yemen—where, as I explained, Iran rules, along with its Houthi friends who attack the government, which was legitimately elected and recognized by the UN—certain Shia groups have been organized. They are not Twelver Shiites but Zaydis (called so by Zayd ibn Ali, the fifth and last legitimate Imam in the local tradition), the same faith as Yemenites, who have always been considered dangerous for their political activism and their tendency to rebel against rulers since the dawn of Islam. Like schoolboys, they go to school to learn the doctrine of the faith of their masters, the Iranians.

## The Nuclear Program of the Islamic Republic

In 2002, a group of dissidents of the National Council of Resistance of Iran (NCRI) revealed details about the country's nuclear program. Iran had signed the Treaty of Non-Proliferation of 1968 and the Safeguard Agreement of 1974. The name of Natanz quickly became well known along with that of Arak: there they had built centrifuges; here they had realized a heavy-water facility where they would be able to produce plutonium. When the world learned about this, Tehran reiterated that it had the "inalienable right to develop nuclear technology" and that the program "was intended for peaceful purposes."

Uranium and plutonium: with these materials Pakistan and North Korea—Iran's mentors in this field—have acquired nuclear weapons. The world quickly realized that, given the stage of development reached by Iran, it was enough to lengthen the enrichment cycle by 25 percent in order to produce fuel suitable for military purposes. It was also evident that the production of plutonium had this purpose, since there was no program for the construction of electric power stations using plutonium. Yet why had all that intense activity been kept a secret? Iran never gave satisfactory answers when asked.

At the time, however, various inspections attested to the fact that Iran was developing the ability to produce fissile material for military use, as Richard Boucher, spokesman for the U.S. State Department, bluntly stated. Colin Powell was courageous, despite the concern of being contested after taking a stance on Saddam Hussein's weapons of mass destruction as well. He said clearly that the Iranians already had missiles that were capable of carrying a nuclear weapon and that now they were working hard on warheads. According to Dore Gold, starting in the 1990s, the Soviet Union had helped Iran to acquire nuclear warhead missiles. In fact, through the secret service, Powell obtained plans in Farsi on how to build just such warheads. In short, for more than two decades Iran was working toward building both nuclear warheads and missiles to carry them. According to the United States, the production of plutonium and highly enriched uranium was a clear signal of the warmongering aims of a country that had no need of alternative energy sources, as they already possessed much oil.

In 2004, pressed by the facts and by ensuing global concern, the International Atomic Energy Agency (IAEA) acquired uranium samples at Natanz and stated that the enrichment implemented could not be part of a civilian project. It also discovered that some nuclear activities were taking place inside military bases. In fact, then Minister of Defense Ali Shamkhani admitted that the army was involved in the enrichment of uranium. What followed, of course, were denials and the circulation of their account about the civilian purpose of the mineral. The insistence on the medical use of radioactive isotopes, which were being produced in large quantities, was almost comical. It reached the point where entire parts of orders were deleted in black ink—orders relative to materials that were necessary for building the bomb, which had been commissioned to foreign companies by the Ministry of Defense.

Iran's nuclear program was for decades an open secret, known to all and, in particular, to the IAEA. Unfortunately, the Egyptian Mohamed Mustafa ElBaradei directed the IAEA for twelve years; a lawyer mysteriously awarded the 2005 Nobel Peace Prize. ElBaradei, with shifty and duplicitous behavior toward Iran, adopted a sophisticated policy of revelations and denials for averting sanctions on the country. It was he, however, who blocked a first attempt at talks when it was revealed that Iran was implementing underground sites and keeping secrets, including a centrifuge plant for the enrichment of uranium and a facility for heavy water.

Europe, however, already had plans to reach an agreement with the Islamic Republic because it wanted to avoid the creation of another coalition and the possible outbreak of war, as happened with Iraq, where it all began with sanctions imposed on Saddam by the UN Security Council. Therefore, the Europeans went to Tehran: the EU-3 (Britain, France, and Germany) tried and in response received the promise from the Iranians that their country would "suspend all of its uranium enrichment and *reprocessing* activities" and allow for more IAEA inspections. However, it became clear pretty quickly that this was only a way to buy time. All spun around the word "suspension," but everyone interpreted it in his own way.

Proof of what was really going on at that time was given by Hassan Rouhani himself, while Europeans, a bit like Obama today, celebrated. Rouhani said: "While we were talking with the Europeans in Tehran, we were installing equipment in parts of the facility in Isfahan." Rouhani also declared that he was pleased with the talks because "We were able to complete the work on Isfahan," to the extent that, at that point, the world would be "forced to take an established fact for granted," which would change "the whole equation." In fact, Rouhani left his post as Secretary of the Supreme National Security Council in 2005, having brought the number of centrifuges from 164 to about 1,500. Today, there are 19,000 centrifuges. The number of centrifuges required to make a bomb in a year is 3,000. Those that remain now in Iranian hands after the agreement are 6,000.

At that moment, Europeans thought they had proven to America that a mild-mannered realist approach could be adopted. However, it didn't happen. Before long, in 2004, Iran declared it would continue to increase the number of centrifuges and, in fact, not allow IAEA inspectors to enter a very important center, which was destroyed instead, removing the land on which it was built so as to avoid the collection of evidence.

Never mind. Europe continued to maintain that in order to push Iran toward the West more goodwill gestures needed to be made. It apparently didn't matter that the regime wouldn't allow inspectors to visit Parchin, the facility where they had experimented with detonators for nuclear weapons. We are very far from the medical use that was claimed for that structure.

To cut a long and disappointing story short: in two years the European project had fallen apart, the promise to suspend enrichment was swiftly abandoned, and the pretentious search for alternative solutions, such as, for example, that of substituting heavy water reactors with light water ones, were deemed "a violation of the agreements by the EU-3."

## Toward the Agreement

Deceit and subterfuge ensued. In 2006, the first anti-Iranian action: sanctions against Iran were approved, along with the additional consent of China and Russia. The aim was to bring the Pasdaran, which controls a business empire that includes military, finance, and insurance industries, to its knees. The decision stipulated that if Iran would be more transparent and accept the conditions of the IAEA, the sanctions would be lifted.

In 2007, Ahmadinejad announced that Iran had begun a program of uranium enrichment on a large scale, with 3,000 centrifuges, enough to produce a bomb in a short time. The president also pointed out that Iran was already in possession of 100 kg of enriched uranium (experts declare this amount is not too far from the quantity needed to make a bomb). The IAEA was alarmed, but the Natanz centrifuges kept spinning. So America got the UN to impose additional sanctions, this time a military embargo.

The Iranian economy falters. Iran thrives on exports of oil and foreign investment. Among the privileged partners of its economy there is also Germany, along with France and China, who themselves suffer a severe blow by the sanctions. The investors start to leave, and products are in short supply because, after further tightening by the UN Security Council, most international transactions are prohibited.

Ahmadinejad, however, is smug. In September 2009, he even came to the brink of armed conflict, because it was discovered that, in secret and always negotiating, Iran had built a second enrichment plant in Fordow, which would allow it to build a nuclear bomb within a few months or even in a few weeks. Asked by the IAEA, which had to report Iran's non-fulfillment, the UN Security Council replied with a *presidential statement* (but not a resolution). It asked the Islamic Republic to stop, while the re-elected Iranian president Ahmadinejad kicked everyone in the face by declaring to the very kind members of the European Union who wanted to continue negotiations that "our people do not need your assistance for development." Everyone condemns, Iran obviously denies, and Khamenei continues his tirades against the West. Meanwhile, the nuclear race continues and Ahmadinejad announces in 2010 that they have begun uranium enrichment programs at 20 percent of purity.

But 2010 is really the year when problems occur: at Natanz centrifuges often stall, so much so that at least a thousand are broken due to continuous fluctuations in their rotor speed. It is the effect of Stuxnet, a computer virus allegedly developed by Israeli and U.S. intelligence in order to sneak into Natanz computers and to literally shut down their computer systems. It is called "Operation Olympic Games," which was initiated by Bush in 2006 and completed by Obama. Despite the latter, however, Iran continues unabated. Following statements, threats, and exchanges of official reports, the IAEA is alarmed: putting together all the uranium enriched at various levels, Iran could be able to produce a bomb.

Obama's America, desperately attempting dialogue, manages to convince China and Russia to support another crackdown on sanctions against Iran. Russia supports Iran but also fears its growing influence in the Middle East and the Caucasus, especially in the states of Persian culture, such as Azerbaijan and Tajikistan. China also fears that Iran will become a power that escapes the world's control, but it is even more afraid that Chinese banks can be affected by the sanctions, and therefore it supports America while looking for a solution through dialogue.

Iran meanwhile is on its knees. The country can now only sell half of the oil that could be placed on the market before the sanctions and the International Monetary Fund predicts that in 2014 it will have to dip into its reserves. Its GDP reaches negative peaks and drops to minus 5 percent. The people, who took to the streets in 2009 and claimed fraud after Ahmadinejad won the elections, are now suffering from the depravations brought about by the sanctions. They protest once again against the regime of the ayatollahs and the insane policy that is leading Iran to misery. The situation risks getting out of the government's control, and therefore the first goal is to try to get the sanctions annulled. This is why Tehran shows itself again "open to dialogue" and will eventually reach the final agreement that promises $150 billion in the first stage alone.

In September 2012, Netanyahu, from the UN podium where he began his political career as an ambassador of Israel, warns the world: with Iran deterrence does not work, because it has a jihadi mentality. Exhibiting a drawing of a bomb, on which he drew a red line, he demanded that there had to be "a clear red line" that Iran cannot cross, because these limits do not cause wars but serve to prevent them! However, negotiations resume with the group of the so-called P5+1, namely, the United States, Russia, China, Great Britain, France, and Germany. Later, Obama will explain that the red line applies only for ten years; afterward, Iran would be free to proceed as it wishes.

While the Iranian press retouches images of Catherine Ashton during negotiations, as they are too revealing for Islamic taste, Iran still challenges the West's patience and announces new centrifuges, new technology, and new uranium. Its nuclear race seems like the behavior of a child who defies his parents, who tell him constantly: "If you don't stop, no games." He insists, and then: "If you don't stop, no dinner." Yet the challenge continues: "If you don't stop, you'll get a slap." However, the child has understood that those threats are empty words and then does whatever he wants to do.

Nevertheless in meetings with the P5+1 and the IAEA, Iran insists it is seeking nuclear power for solely peaceful purposes. It is not ready to make concessions and, in fact, announces new projects and nuclear programs. How could anyone believe in its peaceful aims if every other day Iranian leaders threaten to "eradicate the Zionist cancer," to erase Israel from the face of the earth, and to teach a lesson to the American Satan? In April 2013, everyone leaves the negotiating table with empty hands, while Iran triumphs again and announces a breakthrough in its uranium enrichment programs.

The P5+1, however, continue on the path toward dialogue: after ten years of illusions, pretexts, half-truths, deceptions, and tricks, it seems that the lesson has not been learned. Yet Netanyahu said it: the red line must be established to prevent it, the war! However, the West has grown tired of pulling the rope and lets it go. In November 2013, it reached a temporary agreement—valid for six months—whereby Iran agrees to stop the nuclear program while it will continue negotiations toward a final agreement. This translates into fewer sanctions in exchange for full disclosure of its nuclear sites and a limited amount of enriched uranium. In reality, fewer sanctions are convenient for all. Germany, for example, provides investment in Iran's massive urban infrastructure projects, and the rest of Europe buys its oil and sells their products on the Iranian market.

Here again Tehran takes a step back after having reached out during negotiations. Already in August 2014, after the IAEA's visit to the country, the Iranian Foreign Minister Zarif starts doubting an agreement that should have been final. He is not happy with the restrictive conditions of an eventual deal, while declaring himself "open" to the IAEA. With the same brazenness, he offers Iran's support in the fight against ISIS in return for the lifting of sanctions, albeit helping Bashar Assad with his massacres. Yet again, the Islamic Republic doesn't respect the requests made by the IAEA and the P5+1.

Nevertheless, the negotiations start again under the push of the imperative that "we need to speak to Iran," which, at that time, everyone in Europe regards as the right recipe, even if it is clear that Iran cannot be trusted. Obama rebukes Iran in August, announcing new sanctions, but then proceeds to lift them one by one in order to reach an agreement. Meanwhile, Tehran announces "check," thanks to Europe and Obama's hurry to conclude the game, no matter if at a loss.

Iran doesn't concede on anything, but the negotiations resume. Everyone wants an outcome at any cost. In a few months, in April 2015, the framework for an agreement is already down on paper, contrary to any common sense, and in July it is signed. It marks the darkest page in the history of the West's surrender. Iran celebrates: in defiance of the Great Satan and the hated West, it won the day despite the latter's show of force, reproaches, and threats.

The Vienna Agreement has often been called "historic," and it is, for the misconception of the Iranian interlocutor that it conveys. Who would have thought that an imperialist and Islamic fundamentalist country, a supporter of Hezbollah, Hamas, and the Houthi, and a promoter of horrific terrorist attacks around the world, would have enjoyed an end to the embargo on conventional and ballistic weapons? Moreover, it has reached an agreement that will allow it to recover its atomic program within a few years, and in the open. All this is in exchange for a somewhat uncertain promise on nuclear power. The number of centrifuges and the amount of fissile material that Iran can retain has certainly decreased, but cross-checking the promises that were made is wasted by the conditions set by Minister Zarif: a 24-day notice to visit facilities that his country considers sensitive, and the creation—at the request of Iran—of a commission to establish if they are inspected. It even seems that Iranian inspectors will be the only ones to monitor the Parchin site. Also, there are *snap-back* conditions, i.e., the possibility of bringing back sanctions, which are very hard to implement. As Obama states, it will take 65 days in order to reactivate them, and in any case they will be subject to UN approval. Finally, nothing will prevent Iran from using the $150 billion that will enter its state coffers within one year. As Ayatollah Khamenei has already affirmed in public meetings, "Nothing will change in our policy toward Israel and the United States, our hate is unchanged." So will be Iran's imperialist policy, now much better funded. Khamenei has also been accurately describing the Middle Eastern areas of action, listing countries on a map or hinting at them: Syria, Lebanon, Iraq, Yemen, Jordan, and Palestine. There are those who imagine that Tehran's expansion will serve us in the war against ISIS. However, this hypothesis sounds much like a hope—certainly not a very liberal one—that "they kill each other off." Let us remember that, in the end, there is a basic point on which ISIS and Iran agree: our world is the evil empire, the *dar al-Harb* that Islam will defeat.

CHAPTER 5

## The West's Mistakes

THE WEST IS STRONG and muscular, and it has armies, joint organizations, military equipment tested by countless battles, and first-rate weapons. Yet, the caliph and the ayatollah can win Islam's war in the long run. For the time being, however, they can make our lives hell by putting us constantly on the defensive against possible terrorist attacks.

The fact that the Islamic world has failed in all that we call "modernity" doesn't mean that we know how to defeat it. Modernity is in retreat. Our mind refuses some concepts that are at the crux of modernity: victory, defeat, force, war, open confrontation, hostility of one religion against another, and decisive and armed response in the face of danger to our homes and our children. Not being able to even conceive these ideas, which are the basis of a modern society's dynamics, of its sufferings and of its joys, renders us hesitant and stammering. The Rousseauian Muslim claim that we should go back in time to a different era supersedes our own uncertain existence, which doesn't look back but, at the same time, doesn't even know how to look forward.

In the recent past, we were sure that the terms "modern, democratic, advanced, and progressive" were synonymous with safety. The Second World War, a massacre that left more than

72 million dead and exterminated Jews, Gypsies, and homosexuals, forced upon us a great change of heart. We have made
real progress on the road we've been travelling since the mists
of time, from being *homo* to being truly *sapiens*, conquering
our murderous instincts, our lust for dominance, and our tendency to regard those who are different as inferior beings that
must be crushed.

## The UN and Respect for Human Rights

Human rights, now an undefined mystical expression, have
seemed to us to be the most apparent path, as well as the most
appropriate, to build a kingdom of righteousness on this poor
suffering Earth, plagued by abuses and disparities. Then comes
the UN: at the beginning, right after the war against Hitler,
which had horrified Europe and the United States, it was truly
an alliance built on common principles inspired by these rights.
It is written in its Charter. It's also true that it has included since
the very beginning countries like the Soviet Union and Saudi
Arabia, where human rights were less popular but—with an
implied tolerance on behalf of democratic states for the internal customs of each country, no matter how savage—the idea
was that democracy was still the most desirable common principle, a purpose to achieve and that would one day be reached.

When the General Assembly voted on the Declaration of
Human Rights, the Soviets and Saudis pulled themselves out
of the assembly. But in 1993, only 75 countries out of 184 were
considered democratic, as evidenced by the Freedom House
survey, the research center that measures according to fixed
parameters the level of freedom enjoyed in each country. At
the Durban World Conference against Racism organized in
2001 by the associations for human rights under the auspices
of the UN—I was present and witnessed a shameless display

of anti-Semitism and anti-Americanism, as well as a demonstration that marched while brandishing portraits of bin Laden—the longest standing ovations, to my consternation, went to (and this happened a few days before the attack on the Twin Towers) Fidel Castro, Robert Mugabe, and Yasser Arafat. That's right! The manipulation carried out by the various anti-democratic blocs had reached its goal: to replace the subject of human rights with that of the battle against "American imperialism," "colonial oppression," and "the Zionist occupation."

In 1975, the Arab-Islamic bloc, along with the Soviets and most of the so-called "Non-Aligned" countries (those that flirted with the Soviet Union and harbored a deep resentment toward America), voted for the resolution arguing "Zionism is racism," mysterious in the meaninglessness of its expression. In 1981, the Soviet bloc voted on a resolution entitled "Inadmissibility of Intervention and Interference in the Internal Affairs of States," even, and especially, when it came to human rights. In 1999, Russia sponsored a resolution at the General Assembly to "refrain from the deployment of anti-ballistic missile systems for a defense of the territory of its country." Any military action without UN authorization was ruled illegal, and in addition to condemning the use of force in wars of conquest they quickly passed a condemnation of wars in self-defense except in the unlikely case that the war be authorized by the UN itself. Bush and Thatcher could rely on their own inner convictions and on their determination to proceed anyway, but the mentality from that time to the present day has been formed around this principle. Besides simply attacking national sovereignty, it has eroded the will of the Europeans and the Americans to defend themselves and has left us at the mercy of a community, namely, the UN, where the "Non-Aligned" majority or Islamic sympathizers are now allied with the same anti-Western forces from which it would be necessary to defend themselves.

In the 1970s, the Khmer Rouge killed millions of Cambodians, and no one said anything. Only the Vietnamese invasion put an end to the horrible massacre, just as only India's unilateral decision put an end to the bloody Pakistani conflict, which, in 1971, led to the birth of Bangladesh. Furthermore, only the Tanzanian decision to stop Idi Amin put an end to his criminal campaigns. In the 1990s, the Hutus hacked with machetes more than a million Tutsis in Rwanda, and only the Rwandan Patriotic Front managed to stop them. Meanwhile the UN and the world did next to nothing against that genocide. When the Serbs began to cleanse Bosnia of Muslims and Catholics, it took three years before NATO intervened to stop this genocide. A few years later, in Kosovo, it was again NATO that preempted the plans of ethnic cleansing in Serbia.

The UN was busy approving prudent resolutions while people were being massacred, only to act as world judge once someone else had already stopped the wrongdoers. In the conflict in Congo, which has been called the "Great African War," over five million people were killed and no one intervened to halt the massacres, mutilation, and enslavement of men, women, and children.

What appeared to be a dark legacy of the twentieth century is, again, a reality in this millennium: in Darfur another genocide is occurring, which has so far claimed about half a million victims. We are so determined to call this new genocide "sectarian," but in reality it's once again a Muslim regime that acts against Christians and animists in the south.

The UN has become a body paralyzed by a kind of anti-Western spasm. Anti-Western sentiment is, moreover, the leitmotif of the declarations of the entire world in the war against us. Furthermore, when they call us criminals, murderers, and exploiters there is always some French or American intellectual who agrees.

The ban against criticizing Islam, spread with menacing determination by Muslim countries, has emerged thanks to our cowardice and moral uncertainty. Today, this is certainly the most psychologically relevant phenomenon and full of consequences. This goes in hand with the unbridled condemnation of Israel, a strange and paradoxical phenomenon on account of which the Council for Human Rights devotes 30 percent of its condemnatory resolutions to the State of Israel, while ignoring the countless flaws of the rest of the Middle East, or all the abominations that are happening in China and Africa. All this would make us laugh if it didn't make us cry. The march toward the delegitimization of this country was greatly accelerated by the 2001 conference in Durban, so much so that the use of concepts such as "genocide," "ethnic cleansing," and "apartheid" have become a sign, a wink, a mirage devoid of any real substance, but capable of promoting campaigns based on anti-Semitism and fueled by hatred for the democratic world.

Israel, the subject of so many extravagant and unjust resolutions, was even condemned for the condition of its women, perhaps the most equitable in the world, when Libya chaired the Commission on Human Rights in 2003. Libya, on the other hand, in 2011, when Gaddafi was still in power and the country was on the verge of its descent into chaos, was the subject of warm praise for the internal progress it had made in relation to women's rights.

The European Union has time and again overturned the concept of human rights based on the rules of globalism and multiculturalism, concepts that in themselves ought not to be condemned as they relate to an inescapable contemporary reality. The fact is that their analysis and application suffer from a harmful political censorship. Most of the laws and European institutions act without considering, in fact, that the protagonists of multiculturalism neglect our principle acquisition, democracy, as though it were of little importance. Islamism rejects and despises this value of ours when it suggests that it should be erased in favor of Sharia.

## The Deceptions of Multiculturalism

Yet we show signs of both deep understanding and appeasement. There are almost too many examples of this: Thomas Hammarberg, the Council of Europe's Human Rights Commissioner, came out in favor of the burqa, an unspeakable abomination, in an article in the *Guardian* back in 2010, and again in 2011.

To understand what sort of violation of the dignity of women this constitutes (by our standards, that is, which say that polygamous marriage is an offense and genital mutilation is a crime), just read Khaled Hosseini's novel *A Thousand Splendid Suns*, in which he relates the following scene: "Mariam had never before worn a burqa. Rasheed had to help her put it on. The padded headpiece felt tight and heavy on her skull, and it was strange seeing the world through a mesh screen. She practiced walking around her room in it and kept stepping on the hem and stumbling. The loss of peripheral vision was unnerving, and she did not like the suffocating way the pleated cloth kept pressing against her mouth." Yet, all this doesn't bother the president of the Commission on Human Rights, despite the fact that the first right of a human being is to be oneself, not an anonymous cloth sack, which restricts freedom of movement, annuls personal identity, ruins health, sight, and hearing, and puts mental health in danger, as psychologists explain, having reported serious nervous disorders in those who wear the burqa.

It is immediately evident that the burqa is not a human right, and not a right of women. But out of fear and acquiescence, we have decided to overlook this, just as we have decided to overlook the fact that excision or infibulation are atrocious, and that polygamy puts the man in an intolerable condition of prominence. Nevertheless, Europe has proposed to tolerate and even practice female circumcision in national medical facilities in order to avoid greater physical damage! In 2006, however, the Italian Parliament approved the law that absolutely prohibits this barbaric practice, although some Italian intellectuals, like the philosopher Gianni Vattimo, wanted to officially recognize it in order to reaffirm respect for different cultures.

The Italian Supreme Court has excluded honor killings from our legal codes as a circumstance mitigating punishment under the law. Still, honor killings have returned in vogue in our regions. These are now viewed with lenience by the courts, given that those sisters, daughters, and wives were killed or disfigured by acid in homage to local traditions. Poor Hina Saleem, of Pakistani origin, met her end in this way, killed by her male relatives because she was living with a non-Muslim Italian. So too was Sanaa Dafani, from Morocco, killed by her father for the same grave crime. Furthermore, polygamy is on the rise: in Paris at last half a million people are living in polygamous families, while estimates in Belgium are proportionally similar.

Rampant anti-Semitism falls under the right to freedom of opinion in support for the Palestinian cause, as well as the right to sympathize with terrorist organizations, unless the culprit is caught with the smoking gun in hand. Bilal Bosnić, the Bosnian Salafi imam who came to Italy to preach since at least 2012, was arrested only after having enlisted fifty Muslim recruits in Italy to send to fight in ISIS's ranks. Among these men, some were Italians who had converted to Islam, and two were Bosnian immigrants who lived in the province of Belluno. At least here, it is clear that we are dealing with terrorism. In 2005, on the other hand, an Italian magistrate labeled two Tunisians, Mahar Boujahia and Ali Toumi, as well as a Moroccan, Muhammad Daki, "guerrillas" even though they were recruiting terrorists to send to Iraq. It took another two years before the Italian Supreme Court and then the Senior Criminal Court finally condemned them for terrorism.

Phyllis Chesler, an American writer, psychotherapist, and professor emerita of psychology and women's studies at the College of Staten Island, has written, "Follow the burqa: where you will find it, there is probably habitual violence against women, child abuse, honor killings, polygamy, pathological hatred for Jews, Hindus, Americans, and various infidels." It is not an easy or pleasant thing for security officers at airports or policemen in the streets to inspect a woman who shows so much attachment to modesty, and, in fact, quite a few terrorists have managed in this manner to achieve their aims.

The abandonment of a basic concept of human rights, such as the defense of freedom and democracy, leaves us helpless. We have no moral weapons capable of protecting us from terror. The UN meanwhile has never been able to find a definition of terrorism that would allow them to condemn even the most egregious acts.

In 1982, the General Assembly passed a resolution that cited "the legitimacy of the struggle of peoples against foreign and colonial domination" by all possible means, including armed struggle. This resolution, invoked many times before, allowed the Commission on Human Rights to recognize the "legitimate right of the Palestinian people to resist the Israeli occupation," just after a Hamas terrorist in 2002 assassinated thirty elderly Israelis who were celebrating Passover together at a hotel in Netanya.

No, it is no coincidence that when, in 2006, the young Ilan Halimi was kidnapped in Paris by a gang of Islamist murderers who tortured him to death, the police, as his mother Ruth recounted, refused to follow the trail of anti-Semitic immigrants, attributing the attack to common criminality. Law enforcement agencies, following the direction of political correctness, still in vogue in France today, did not want to be accused of Islamophobia.

This attitude blinds us in front of our main enemy, terrorism. It is not by chance that the Al-Aqsa Intifada, which began in 2001 and has since claimed more than a thousand victims in Israel, in cafés, on buses, and in supermarkets, was scandalously ignored by the media and international organizations, while condemnations of its leaders were rare and formal, all while the slaughter of Jews, men, women, and innocent children, was underway.

## Europe and the Islamic Question

It would take very long to go through all the stages of how Europe has turned multiculturalism into a habit of silence and reluctance that has changed its cultural and political connotations. A mix of energetic appetite, fear of terrorism, and an old, dear friend, anti-Semitism, disguised as criticism of the State of Israel, led the EEC to opt for an unconditional integration policy with the Arab world, which foresaw a true unification of the two sides of the Mediterranean.

Bat Ye'or writes in her book *Eurabia* that the European Community has adopted this policy since 1967, after the Six-Day War, sustaining it with a gigantic propaganda machine that has infiltrated national parliaments, trade unions, industries, and cultural centers. Countless milestones have marked this road. It is enough to recall however that, after 1967, the Association de Solidarité Franco-Arabe was founded in France with the participation and encouragement of ministers, diplomats, and intellectuals, as well as Bishop Maurice Couve de Murville and the director of the left-wing Catholic newspaper *Témoignage*

*Chrétien*, Georges Montaron. In England, a sister organization was born, and little by little other large machines of consensus and integration appeared. Finally, the Second International Conference for the Support of the Arab Peoples, held in 1969, united intellectuals like the historian Arnold Toynbee, French minister Louis Terrenoire, and the famous Arabist Jacques Berque. Of the 54 members of the organizing committee, 44 of whom were European, 33 were Western European and 11 were from communist countries. The result of this committee, according to the author, was driven by a strong determination, which continues to this day, to combine pro-Palestinian policy with an invitation to the Arab world to be part of Europe, a policy that—of course—favors immigration.

In the years following Europe's choice to promote this policy, terrorism, especially Palestinian, increased dramatically with plane hijackings against El Al, Swissair, and TWA, with letter bombs to diplomats, the massacre of Israeli athletes in Munich in 1972, the bursts of machine gun fire on Christians visiting Lod, and the murder of Leon Klinghoffer, for the mere fact that he was Jewish, aboard the *Achille Lauro*.

But the agreement between Europe and the Arab countries has not cracked, and even today the effort of continuous rehabilitation with the Muslim world follows down the path of international terrorism while Europe looks the other way.

Thanks to the policy of dialogue, thousands of mosques and "charitable" Islamic organizations have opened, often funded with money from Saudi Arabia and Qatar, and in any case with the help of external forces beyond those of the immigrants. From these pulpits they often preach the most aggressive principles of the Quran, exerting a fundamental religious influence in their host countries. Young people are literally recruited and dragged into the sea of confusion of Islam, which enraptures them with its international branches.

Anti-Semitism had experienced a strong flare-up until it resulted in murderous episodes, while the Islamic centers, instead of facilitating the integration of immigrants in Europe, sometimes distribute propaganda books such as *The Protocols of the Elders of Zion* and *Mein Kampf* in Arabic and Urdu.

If we wonder how things will proceed now that terrorism has gone berserk and besieges us in our own home, we can find the answer in the crystal ball of eroded thought. The Venice Biennale of 2015 opened in May with the presentation of a work of art by Iceland's representative, Christoph Büchel: he temporarily converted an old Venetian church that had been closed for some time, Santa Maria della Misericordia, into a mosque. The event raised no objection but, rather, generated a certain satisfaction among the authorities, who saw it as a sign of "hospitality," a word that has become a value in itself, as if the person, the thing, and the ideas to be accepted had no importance. Come on in!

And so they entered, not just the immigrants in need and deserving of help, but also those who then set fire to Europe. For example in 2005, when the Danish newspaper *Jyllands-Posten* dared to publish cartoons on Muhammad, violent protests broke out in the Muslim world, during which at least 200 innocent people were killed, while churches were set ablaze and shops were vandalized.

In 2015, when the PEN American Center, the U.S. branch of PEN International (the association of writers that promotes freedom of expression and the defense of intellectuals persecuted for their opinions), decided to give an award to *Charlie Hebdo*, there was a violent reaction—some would say crazy—on the part of some writers in the jury who decided to distance themselves. It is known that *Charlie Hebdo* suffered an attack on January 7, 2015, due to its publication of caricatures considered anti-Islamic. Twelve editors were killed in this attack (even writing this I can barely believe my own words). What could possibly exist that is more supportive of freedom of thought than *Charlie Hebdo*?

Instead Peter Carey, Francine Prose, Michael Ondaatje, Rachel Kushner, Taiye Selasi, and Teju Cole (we write their names to engrave their shame here) felt that, in actuality, the award should go to Islamophobia. What a perversion of the intellectual mind! Peter Carey has gone so far as to express his support not for *Charlie Hebdo* but for the Islamic minority in France. On Carey, the former U.S. representative to the UN John Bolton wrote, "We did not hear protest when Ilan Halimi was tortured to death for weeks." Even Salman Rushdie criticized Carey and the others, despite himself being a writer who has never had the enthusiastic support of his colleagues. In fact, his fellow writers had in the past boycotted his book *The Satanic Verses* while he was (as he still is today) the victim of a *fatwa* that condemns him to death.

These episodes by now are continuous in America and in Europe. Rushdie's *The Satanic Verses* provoked a series of events and later crimes all over Europe. Islam terrorizes while pretending to induce good feelings by challenging the racism of Islamophobia: behold the power of the myth of human rights. For example, the University of Maryland has prohibited the viewing of the film *American Sniper* by Clint Eastwood because it disturbs Muslims; a conference on the attack upon *Charlie Hebdo* was canceled at the University of Belfast; the publication of the book *The Jewel of Medina* by Sherry Jones was canceled in 2008 by Random House, which had bought the rights to the book, and later her new publisher's house was set on fire.

The University of California, Berkeley, in an effort to render the censorship of even critical analyses of Islam more sophisticated, has organized six international conferences on Islamophobia and now publishes an academic journal entitled

*Islamophobia Studies Journal.* To think that the founder of the Department of Islamic Studies at Berkeley, Munir Jiwa, continues to claim that the West sees Islam, terrorism, Sharia, and the oppression of women solely through the prism of religion. According to him, all of this is the result of a geopolitical contingency and identifying Islam as the root of these problems is Islamophobic.

But the deepest wounds in the Western consciousness, quickly metabolized like fresh water, were the murders of Dutch filmmaker Theo Van Gogh in 2004 and of the Dutch politician Pim Fortuyn in 2002, as well as numerous other murders or attempted murders, such as the threats against women's rights activist Ayaan Hirsi Ali. Even I, since 2001, when the Second Intifada began, have had to be protected by a security escort.

The background noise of these murders has been the violent marches that accompany every defense campaign carried out by Israel to defend itself against Gaza. Although it is quite clear that Israel has always acted reluctantly and as a result only of endless rocket attacks on its cities carried out by Palestinians in connection with Hamas, attacks that reached even Tel Aviv and its kibbutzim, and that asymmetric warfare, in which the missile launchers were hidden in homes and hospitals, forced dire military measures that endangered first and foremost Israeli soldiers. Notwithstanding these facts, anti-Semitic hatred has touched new heights. Even in the streets of Berlin they sang the words "Hamas, Hamas, Jews to the gas!" I will say here that I think the misunderstanding over the Israeli–Palestinian conflict is one of the principal sources of corruption of the Western mind. Additionally, they continue to believe that this conflict is the source of all other conflicts in the Middle East. This hypothesis makes no sense, and delays any reasonable reaction, but it is repeated like a comfortable old refrain, thereby diverting our attention from the Shiite–Sunni confrontation.

For people who believe that after millennia of philosophy and good will, from the Greeks to Maimonides, Erasmus to Kant, a certain sensibility should have brought us to a state of tolerance and a path to peace, it may seem strange that a personality belonging to the mainstream, like the Archbishop of Canterbury, would come out strongly in support of the introduction of Sharia law in Britain, along with Muslim courts operating in parallel with the state judicial system. It might also seem strange that, in the wake of anti-Israeli demonstrations, Ken Livingstone, Mayor of London from 2000 to 2008, invited (and passionately embraced) Yusuf al-Qaradawi to speak in his city, a Sunni cleric who defines Palestinian suicide bombers as "martyrs." This happened a year before the immense explosion in London's underground in 2005, which resulted in 52 deaths and left hundreds injured. All this after entire neighborhoods had become impossible for women to enter with short sleeves and knee-length skirts because they are *Sharia-controlled zones*, i.e., neighborhoods patrolled by Sharia patrols.

But in London, these Islamic colonies, outside of the control of the state, were not enough to make the British open their eyes. Neither was the fatal stabbing of the 25-year-old soldier Lee Rigby on the streets of London in 2013, assaulted, as I have already said, by two British converts to Islam, sons of Nigerian immigrants.

It's clear that all over Europe a patchwork of increasingly numerous enclaves where the light of Western intellect has no power is opening wide breaches in which the terrorist strategy of the caliphate and Islamic imperialism have good chances of penetrating and winning, especially through violence, the same violence that we abhor and refuse not only to use but even to consider.

Encrusted over the agitation in Europe provoked by a new, large Muslim presence, there exists (still today) anti-imperialist, anti-American, and anti-Semitic hatred, which the radical left has never abandoned, a remnant from the days when Moscow saw Israel as the long arm of the United States (as it was during the Cold War). New anti-European right-wing groups have themselves started to forge close relationships with the anti-Semitic Islamic presence in Europe, as in the days of Hitler. This can be seen in the behavior of Jean-Marie Le Pen, the old National Front leader, who has become a close friend of the anti-Semite Dieudonné, whose long career as a comedian and anti-racism activist has not prevented him from joining the French far right.

The foundation of the West's fears is not far-fetched. In fact, 23 percent of the world's population is Muslim, that is, 1.6 billion people. Certainly not all of them are extremists, but when you check how many of them desire the establishment of Sharia law, you will get amazing results. If we take, for example, the simple support of ISIS, for all its extreme ferocity, we discover, through research by the Washington Institute for Near East Policy commissioned by the *New Republic*, that 3 percent of Egyptian adults approves of ISIS, i.e., in that country it has a following of a million and a half people. The percentage touches 5 percent in Saudi Arabia (and we are still talking about anti-ISIS countries), amounting to half a million people, while in Lebanon 1 percent sympathize with the Islamic State.

It's enough to create a sea of serious troubles. Approval ratings for other terrorist groups are also very high. For example, in Egypt, despite the fact that al-Sisi has outlawed it, a third of the population favors Hamas, while the figure is 52 percent in Saudi Arabia. The Muslim Brotherhood has an approval rating of 35 percent in Egypt and 32 percent in Saudi Arabia. In Lebanon, opinion is strongly affected by religious divisions, but sympathy for Hezbollah is nonetheless remarkable: among the

Shiites it is 92 percent, while among Christians it reaches 40 percent. Alas, the mysteries of the human soul.

The West, in particular the United States, is not at all popular, while on the other hand support for Sharia remains very high. According to a survey by the Pew Research Center, the majority of the population in Arab countries is in favor of making Sharia the state law. This includes nearly 90 percent of Palestinians, more than 90 percent of Iraqis, and 74 percent of Egyptians. Even in countries such as Malaysia and Indonesia, as well as Kenya and Ethiopia, the majority of the population wants the dictates of the Quran to be state law. The same applies to a disturbing 15 percent in Bosnia. If you examine those who think that Sharia should also apply to non-Muslims, the data is even more frightening: for example, 44 percent of Egyptians, 30 percent of Bosnians, and 44 percent of Palestinians are in favor of imposing the yoke of Islamic law even on infidels.

## "Foreign Fighters," the West's Children

The Islamic presence in our countries brings with it, often for purely ideological reasons or family ties, a visceral spirit of vindication, of anti-Western victimhood, and even, in many cases, the desire to dominate. This attitude becomes a televised debate, while confused and furious youth protest through blogs, instant messaging, and social networks on the Internet. In this way we come across statistics that might take us aback, but which speak to us of the future. It's not just "random" cells (as Obama would say). Fifteen percent of French youths between the ages of eighteen and twenty-four have a positive attitude toward the Islamic State. In England, ISIS sympathizers are 11 percent, and in Germany it's 10 percent. These percentages, which decrease with age, are due to the increase of the Muslim population in a Europe that continues to refuse to have children, while the Muslims, who were 4.1 percent in 1990, have become 6 percent today. In 2030, they will be 58 million, i.e., 8 percent of the European population according to the Pew Research Center.

In Europe and America, therefore, an army of foreign fighters, converted immigrants or second- or third-generation ones, constitute a fifth column, active and fearsome, of terrorists departing or returning: they are the fighters of ISIS's army, indoctrinated through and through, not only in cultural centers but also on the Internet. These are young men we can meet on the street or at work, students or colleagues, smiling and elegant. Sometimes they may be marginalized gang members, such as those who killed Halimi. Often they are simply young people who feel unfulfilled, who want to have a role, a voice, a purpose in life, and to express themselves through a big project.

Of the young jihadists born within our community who have decided to dedicate their lives to destroying them, we fear above all else their return home after a stint in Syria or Iraq in ISIS's ranks. Intelligence agencies consider it one of the most serious threats that loom over the future of Europe because what was once considered a curious whim of a few fanatics has now become the choice of many people. By now 20,000 people have crossed borders, passing in general via Turkey. This data, reported by the *Washington Post*, was provided by the International Centre for the Study of Radicalization and Political Violence (ICSR) in January 2015. When they return, loaded and trained (unless they have fled from the front), they are ready to be used as domestic terrorists.

The conflict in Syria has attracted more foreign combatants than the war in Afghanistan during the 1980s, when many Muslims responded to the call of jihad against the Soviet Union. The last conflict for which so many young people have moved far from home was the one against Hitler in 1945. One fifth of foreign fighters come from Western countries, and their numbers are rapidly increasing. France has tripled the number of its fighters, increasing from 412 in 2013 to 1,200 in 2014. In Belgium, a small country but perhaps the most fiercely Islamic, they rose from 269 to 440. In Germany, recruiters are successful. The latter are highly specialized figures, well trained and conspicuously funded, able to preach unhindered and with great frankness in Islamic structures that Western countries refuse to control.

Among those leaving for Syria there are numerous women: they are teenagers and good students. They are like Kadiza Sultana, Shamima Begum, and Amira Abase, who departed on February 17, 2015, from London's Gatwick Airport to Turkey and from there passed into Syria; one of them with her head covered, and all three wearing trousers. Three girls who left their families astonished, their mothers in tears, and their fathers in anger. This was also the case for the family of 17-year-old Sahra Mehenni, whose father accompanied her, as he did every morning, to the Lézignan-Corbières station, in France, to send her off to school. Instead, she decided to abandon her Muslim-Catholic family with five children for a new home in the north of Syria to pursue jihad, perhaps even death, and the pure love of an arranged marriage with one of the purest and perhaps most fascinating warriors of Allah.

Side by side with the fighters, who are won over by a simpler message of war and martyrdom, ISIS encourages women to establish themselves in this state-in-the-making. Women, after all, are the pillars of the infrastructure of Islamic society. A new online group affiliated with ISIS, Al-Zawra'a, has posted a series of videos aimed at women. It explains how to handle weapons and fight, and it suggests that they learn to cook halal from their mothers and to sew fighter's uniforms. The videos also give first aid lessons in order to help the wounded, and explain that women will need to sew and cook until Allah chooses them for martyrdom.

The girls they recruit come from all over the world and offer themselves up for any task, including guards for the brothels where women slaves, as permitted by ISIS's Sharia rules, are raped. Their escape from the West is, however, the consequence, and we must never forget it, of an essentially friendly environment, in London or Paris, where they were able to cultivate their fundamentalist ambitions. Their desire for identity has not been met by democratic models transmitted by motivated teachers, but only by an uncertain confusion of globalist models seasoned by the fight against "Islamophobia" that dominates Western society.

"I miss you Mom and Dad," writes Sahra. "I eat well, I'm fine. I am aware of the choice I have made. I have not gone blind. I love you very much, *mes amours!*" Her brother says that the messages have over time become increasingly short and broken. Maybe Sahra is tired, or perhaps those romantic fighters with their hair blowing in the wind and sabers in their hands, these heroes of Islam so similar to Muhammad's warriors, have become absent husbands, severely obsessive in their religious demands. Perhaps they have taken concubines or wives, convinced as they are that woman is a lesser being than man, especially if that man is a warrior. Or they have simply become corpses, soldiers killed in a fierce war, turning these poor girls into miserable Sharia widows.

## The War against Modernity

Contrary to what political analysts who believe in integration maintain, Islam's inability to be "modern," as already mentioned, places it in the wake of the most current trends, and puts it on the highest crest of the wave. Because modernity, which political Islam abhors, along with its favorite form of society, democracy with gender equality, has fallen into a serious crisis, as I have said.

The pillars of our international system, from the Treaty of Westphalia in the seventeenth century to the United Nations today, tremble and crumble. Since the end of the Cold War they have tried to eliminate national borders in the vain hope of establishing a common identity that fits all—even those who do not accept their basic principles—and human rights have been transformed into a tool to attack the West and not for defending the weak. However appeasement of fundamentalist Islam has become more ideological in recent years.

Even though our willingness to allow Islam to bully us was already there, Obama has translated this attitude into policy. Every occasion is a good one for repeating that Islam is a religion of peace and that its attacks are in fact random gestures, not related to faith but rather to some deplorable attitude induced by insanity, or worse yet, the result of the suffering caused by a sick society, unable to accommodate the unfortunate at home.

Today, we have in the United States the mainstay of a policy that refuses to recognize Islam as a danger and not merely one of the major world religions. The steps taken since the beginning of Obama's presidency express a great, and certainly laudable, dedication to peace. Already in his inaugural speech Obama made friendship with the Muslim world a cornerstone of his presidency and denounced the wrong tone of the public debate toward its components. In 2009, at the NATO summit in Strasbourg, he called for people to overcome differences and show more respect for Islam. He then made a visit to Turkey and affirmed before its parliament that America wants closer relations with Islam, capable of going beyond the fight against terrorism, in the belief that it is possible to free Islamic political violence from the ideology that created it. But Cairo is where Obama introduced his project for rapprochement with Islam, speaking at Al-Azhar University, the Vatican of Sunni Islam. On this occasion, Obama defined Islam as a religion of peace, liberty, tolerance, and progress, values, he says, that Islam shares with America. The president refrains however from talking about the status of women, commending rather the political careers of some women in Indonesia, Pakistan, and Turkey. Obama has proven that he aspires to a world in which Islam and the West share almost everything. He also subscribes to the view that the West has always scorned and offended Islam, crushing it with colonialism. In his interpretation of things, terrorism loses the primary role it played in the policies of his predecessors. The president neither dwells on the persecution of minorities nor insists on individual freedom.

If Obama had not opted from the beginning of his first term for a policy of pacification with Islam in all its variegated forms, and had he not believed that his legacy should be, at all costs, the harmonious coexistence of cultures, our world would be different now.

Obama's Middle East policy is the result of his beliefs and of his cultural and ideological approach. At first, during the Arab Spring uprisings, he even tried to open the doors of international diplomacy to the Muslim Brotherhood, who do not hide their project of Islamization. However, the great Middle East tsunami doesn't seem to forgive anyone, neither ISIS on the one hand nor Iran's hegemonic ambitions on the other. Obama is convinced, as is Europe, that an apologetic and understanding attitude is the first step toward dialogue. Of course it's natural that it should be this way. Our world is based on critical thought, which brings about self-analysis and the admission of one's own faults. However, in Islamic political culture this *mea culpa* is a sign of the subjugation of the infidel Western world.

Let's be clear, I am not at all in favor of war. The blood, massacres, and violence that Europe and America have experienced in order to build a free world in continuous improvement should be enough for centuries to come. However, I believe that, precisely out of the respect for cultures and diversity, Europe and America should begin to understand that not everyone thinks like us, that other cultures have different historical and ideological references and dissimilar aspirations. This is certainly the case with Islam, which sees the world differently and with diverse historical references. It always feels attacked by us Westerners, by us Crusaders, us colonialists, us free and critical thinkers. Therefore, when we recite these apologies, seeking the goodwill of the Muslim world, we actually create the opposite effect. Namely, we increase the feeling of dominance and presumption that has its roots in an alleged historical injustice. All or most studies on Islamic culture tell us that Islam imposes advancement on any ground from which we retreat.

What is most worrying is that a critical approach, the key that advances our thinking and is the basis of our way of life, is silenced by the fear of Islamophobia. But if we are obliged to criticize and analyze the mistakes made by the West with colonialism, if we can and we want to challenge the ideologies that the West has produced and we are ready to condemn our extremes, why can't we do the same with the Islamic world? Why do we feel compelled to make an act of contrition for colonialism, but, if we speak of Islamic expansionism, we are accused of Islamophobia? Why can secular Western satire ridicule, mock, and mistreat religious Christians and Jews, but if you dare to do the same in relation to Islamic ones then it is called Islamophobic? We want the separation of church and state, a pillar of our social concept, but we are not willing to say no to Sharia because we are afraid of being accused of racism.

Putting our heads in the sand, hoping that a "moderate" Islam would manifest itself thanks solely to multiculturalism, was a big mistake. It has allowed fundamentalism to grow in Europe and has given birth to movements throughout the world whose utmost aspiration is to impose Sharia law. If politicians and authorities had publicly identified the enemy in Islamic fundamentalism and if they had fought it without hesitation in the mosques, in the suburbs, and in the dens of proselytes, we surely would have been more effective in helping moderate Muslims acquire strength and appear in public without fear.

Both Iran, with its hegemonic aims, and ISIS, with its extremist frenzy, pursue the project of imposing Islam upon the world, starting with the Middle East and coming to the West, where the free propaganda in mosques and Islamic centers attracts youths who, tired of jeans, universities, and nightclubs, prefer Sharia and jihad.

Yet in all this chaos we can see a way out. A new political will is emerging, a project for a new Middle East and a new relationship with Islam. We will see in the next chapter how it is possible to escape this quagmire in which we have been led by *appeasement* and other presumptuous errors of a ruling class and a frightened public.

CHAPTER 6

## If Not Love, at Least Mutual Respect

SEVENTY-ODD YEARS AGO, the world was faced with an enemy that represented evil in its purest form: in the name of its credo, it killed, tortured, and made slaves of men and women, young and old. Defeating it was possible only by destroying it at the source. The war was terrible and ruthless, but in the end German Nazism and Japanese imperialism had to surrender. Later, a hard battle in the name of freedom was to be waged against communism as well, an ideology sharing many features with Nazism. The struggle to defeat communism, however, was far more drawn out and complex. Its hegemonic supremacy, its power of persuasion in the West, as well as its enormous activism in creating fifth columns (communist parties, collateral organizations for women, youths, professionals, sports groups, and intellectuals of whose activities we still see traces today) all required a great deal of intense military, diplomatic, and cultural action on behalf of the West.

Given everything we have said thus far, it seems very unlikely that the West will be able to successfully engage in the war against today's representation of evil, jihadism, both Sunni and Shia, which hold us as in a vice; two forms, one no less dangerous than the other, and, furthermore, in conflict even with each other.

For the moment, the prevailing trend of Western democracies is that of the desperate search for a peaceful way out, some form of *appeasement*, unlike Russia, which prefers a different approach. Looking around us, it seems very difficult to identify any power with the determination and charisma to coordinate a planned defense against all forms of radical Islam, from the Iranian Shia who control Syria, Iraq, Yemen, and Lebanon to the Sunni of the Muslim Brotherhood, Erdoğan, Qatar, and ISIS.

Today, the West is morally and strategically against an armed war. Who on earth would feel ready to take up arms in vast and uncertain territories in order to win a war against ISIS? Moreover, everyday we continuously hear reports of battles being lost or skirmishes over this or that city in a constant back-and-forth when all it would take is one well-armed modern military division to go in there and send all the caliph's men running.

The American choice, which is what matters most at present, is a strict refusal to put *boots on the ground*, i.e., to send ground troops, while instead agreeing to provide drone coverage for the military operations of the deft Kurdish Peshmerga. Or, in dire situations, the United States will decide to defend places that are about to fall into the hands of Islamists or to win them back. The clashes around the city of Ramadi, for example, have been going on for months, and this battle, just like that of Kobane, is a decisive battle to crush ISIS. And yet, the United States has hesitated to take the steps to win the city once and for all. Now the Americans have sent 450 military advisers to be stationed at the base of Al-Taqaddum. They will not actually engage in combat, but they will provide strategic support to Iraqi soldiers.

ISIS isn't invincible. The Kurdish Peshmerga, which first fought against Saddam, who wanted to exterminate them in the 1980s, and which are now are fighting against ISIS, have proven this. They want to carve out an independent state for themselves, and they battle to defend their people, persecuted by the Arabs, as well as by the Iranians and the Turks. In the 1990s, they opened their army to women, who throw ISIS's cutthroats into a panic because dying at the hands of a female hand precludes their ascent to heaven. They have a special relationship with Israel: the Kurdish press speaks of the Jewish state in positive terms, it raises awareness about Israeli culture and society, and it identifies with Israel's efforts in combating terrorism.

Furthermore, the Islamic State's forces are scattered over their territory, necessitating military intervention in the form of thousands of bombardments. They must also use caution not to hit the civilian population in order to avoid the inevitable worldwide condemnation that comes with asymmetric warfare. Unfortunately, there is always the risk that some innocents will be harmed whenever the enemy is attacked, given that terrorists and fighters always hide among civilians.

Israelis have been criticized by the world press for having targeted neighborhoods, mosques, and (empty) schools in Gaza where weapons, used to bomb even Tel Aviv, were being hidden. They have faced criticism as well for destroying homes that had been converted into barracks for Hezbollah. Today, there are even calls to prosecute the Israelis for war crimes. Naturally, Obama's drones are subject to similar condemnation.

Even when terrorists are identified, a thousand precautions prevent us from stopping them. In order to arrest and prosecute them they must be captured "with the smoking gun in hand" because, even if the intelligence agencies identified them while they were organizing a military expedition in Syria, they will always find a judge who sends them back home. It is forbidden, after all, to use evidence obtained in a security investigation.

## Illusions and Possibilities

So guerilla warfare appears to be ruled out at the present. It wouldn't be impossible to confront and defeat ISIS's bearded armies, just as it wouldn't be impossible to impede Iran's imperialistic moves. However, many precautions make a winning strategy difficult. We've seen examples of this in some of the most important battles, like Ramadi, where the fight against ISIS was lost and they were given free reign just a few kilometers outside Baghdad. This is what happened after months of clashes and intense strategic meetings that focused on a relatively small number of drone attacks (3,800 in eight months against the 47,000 launched in the first month of Operation Iraqi Freedom in 2003) in support of an Iraqi army that was unable to fight due to sectarian erosions and the fear of ISIS. The tentative prospect of allowing the Iranians to fight ISIS instead of the paralyzed Iraqi army leaves us leery as well. What a nice prospect if the cities now in the hands of ISIS became Iranian in the event of an Iranian victory.

No, military solutions don't work, or at least they won't work as long as Assad's presence paralyzes any intervention. In fact, defeating ISIS would mean helping this savage dictator, responsible for the deaths of over 200,000 people, and doing a conspicuous favor for Iran. On the other hand, helping Assad in the fight against ISIS would be an excessive reversal of all of Obama's initial positions.

Nevertheless, it is through reading the news of the last three years we can begin to devise a hypothesis for containment (that in itself is something, even if it doesn't promise "pacification"), which would be very difficult to pursue but is promising nonetheless, provided that we give up our illusions and our prejudices. These can be summarized in three points.

The first and most important point is the belief that instability in the Middle East stems from the Israeli–Palestinian conflict. Nothing is more stupid and blatantly false. (If there were a Palestinian state, would it perhaps decrease beheadings by ISIS? Or would it change anything in the Saudi war against the pro-Iranian Houthi in Yemen?) Perhaps the dumbest idea of all is that Palestinian antagonism and hatred toward Israel only started in 1967, when the Six-Day War resulted in Israel occupying the Jordanian territory of the West Bank. It is enough to consider the list of Palestinian terrorist attacks against Jewish communities during the Mandate of Palestine or the record of nationalist hatred by Haj Amin al-Husseini, the Grand Mufti of Jerusalem, who allied with Hitler, or even the outbreak of war against the 1948 partition, in order to understand that this idea is simply a fairy tale. Before 1967, the anti-Jewish apparatus was already fully in motion. After all, in 1948, the Arab states rejected a division between Israel and Palestine and decided to attack Israel in an attempt to throw it back into the sea, just as they would probably do today if they had reached an agreement … but that's another story.

The second point is the illusion that negotiation, and therefore compromise, is possible with Islamic extremists. For political Islam, nothing is more prohibited than peace with the enemy. Such a thing is not envisioned in the Quranic code of conduct. Proof of this is Khamenei's insistence on the obligatory hatred against the United States, which he reiterated during the recent nuclear negotiations. One cannot practice compromise while one practices *hudna*, a temporary cease-fire, which means neither peace nor truce but instead usually serves for rearming oneself and resuming war. Thus, for us, we may think that we have reached a peace agreement only to find ourselves tragically deceived.

In Arabic there are several words that translate our concepts of "truce," "peace," and "armistice." There is the *'ahd,* a truce that implies an understanding with the enemy and reconciliation, while *sulh* translates into Arabic our concept of "peace treaty." Well, the Arab press uses mostly the word *hudna* even when it speaks about the Armistice lines of 1949, which now have become the 1967 borders. Even bin Laden, in 2006, had offered Bush a *hudna,* a prerogative of a Muslim ruler.

The *hudna* entered into the Islamic conceptual repertoire in the Quranic episode of the false truce that Muhammad had agreed to in 628 with the Quraysh tribe, who controlled Mecca. After two years of reorganization and rearmament, the Quraysh displeased Muhammad, and that was enough for him to destroy them. That's how *hudna* works: just one little excuse, or one misstep in this wobbly arrangement—which barely even amounts to a real agreement—is enough to resume jihad!

The other problematic assumption is that you can pitch one form of extremism, Shiite Iran, against the other, Sunni ISIS. It is evident that such a strategy only yields an expansion of Iranian imperialist strength, as is already happening in Syria, Iraq, Yemen, and Lebanon, while ISIS continues to thrive. A proxy war won't work; we aren't going to find an Iranian force that works for the West. As part of his legacy, Obama wants to leave an Iran that will be the bearer of a new equilibrium. Instead, Iran will continue to bring discord, being both unpopular in all the Middle East and a source of Sunni protest.

Finally, the third point: you have to understand that there does not exist, hidden inside some mosque, a mass of moderate Muslims who are ready to run to our aid, or at least to condemn and eventually block the "bad guys." Surely, a part of the Muslim world wants peace and a quiet life. After all, with all due respect, a Muslim is a product of the world he lives in;

it isn't that he's a bad person. ISIS and Iran, in their respective areas, are not seen as extremists that must be condemned, but solely as sources of a burning dilemma. ISIS, in fact, carries out all of Sharia's rules to the letter. Iran, too, has created an Islamic Republic with deep-seated rules in Islamic law. Sharia is taught in schools and universities, as well as at home in the family. It is taught to every religious Muslim, and it's inscribed in his culture and in his heart. It's difficult for us to understand, but the strict rules for diet and clothing, the subjugation of women, and even stonings, crucifixions, beheadings, the killing of pagans (like the Yazidis), or the enslavement of women are all rules written in the Quran, and a good Muslim, even if he is an individual who abhors blood, might wonder whether the new phenomena of ISIS and of an Iran in expansion won't bring about a just upholding of Sharia in its original terms.

In October 2014, Zvi Mazel, former Israeli ambassador to Romania, Egypt, and Sweden, told the story about a distinguished professor of Islamic law and economics, Dr. Iman Mustafa al-Bugha, who resigned from the University of Dammam in Saudi Arabia in order to join the armies of Islamic State in northern Syria. He recounted in the *Jerusalem Post* what she wrote on her Facebook page: "The moment I realized the tragedies of the Muslim people, I became a member of the Islamic State, even before ISIS was created…Jihad is the way, the true way. Its leaders cannot change a thing on its way to a just victory and if al-Baghdadi were to stray from this path we would replace him; the true way—the Jihad—lights the path of the true believers who abandoned the world and its dissolute ways to fulfill their duty until death."

It's simple. This is confirmed by many writings and positions taken despite the incessant attempt to reiterate that jihad, those calling to arms, and Sharia, those of obedience to the written rules that force them to kill and decapitate, are not "true Islam." It is misguided to hope for moderate Islam, to invoke it, or to ask it to strike a blow against extremism.

Therefore, if we eliminate the route of guerilla warfare because it no longer corresponds to the aspirations or anthropology of the contemporary world as we see it, we must also avoid hoping that a bunch of courageous moderates, or staunch dissidents, are willing to be considered apostates by their fellow Muslims. Very few imams or spiritual leaders, and no Muslim politician, will go beyond the immediate condemnation of a particularly savage attack. They will quickly add that such acts aren't in any way representative of Islam. Meanwhile, those who rightfully call for reform are considered black sheep.

## Getting to Know Islam

So if we are determined to find a realistic path to take, we should look at things the way a Muslim would, i.e., with his interests in mind and how these interests might be threatened. Let us remember what Professor Bernard Lewis said to justify the seemingly incomprehensible move by Anwar al-Sadat to make peace with Israel (a move that cost him his life). He explained that the decision was made when Egypt, as a result of the Soviet Union's decline, suddenly felt abandoned by its best ally and resolved therefore to protect itself from the greatest danger, i.e., a strong Israel backed by the United States, the same Israel that won a crushing defeat against Egypt in the Six-Day War. Thus, in an unthinkable act, Sadat signed the Camp David Accords.

Today, the situation in the eyes of the Arab States that we would define as moderates is pretty much the same. For decades they have been *contractors*, allies of American power, in one way or another, and feel themselves now abandoned and betrayed by Obama, who, after having made it clear with his actions, went on to openly say the following during a summit with Saudi Arabia, Oman, Kuwait, UAE, Bahrain, and Qatar held at Camp David and Washington on May 14, 2015: "We do not want to isolate Iran. We want an Iran that, responsibly, plays a role in the region." According to his doctrine, in fact, an agreement with Iran will be a great help in maintaining equilibrium in the Middle East.

Six Arab countries had already expected the Iranian deal and American foreign policy's subsequent settlement, and they were prepared. The Saudi King Salman decided not to show up and sent dignitaries in his place. Bahrain also made it known that King Hamad al-Khalifa would not participate. Therefore, among the six countries invited, the only two monarchs present were the emirs of Qatar and Kuwait. Given his life story, U.S. President Obama, the son of a mixed culture, would like to project onto the entire world the good fortune he has had in feeling the fusion between the Christian world and the Muslim world as perfectly natural.

In the Middle East, the immense interests of Riyadh have been undermined. Iran is the Saudi monarchy's main concern, especially now that the pro-Iranian Houthi military occupies much of Yemen, threatening therefore their country and seeking control of the Mandab Strait, through which three-quarters of international shipping traffic passes. Salman's decision not to go to Obama's summit demonstrates that relations with the United States have shifted.

The request that the American president made to Sunni heads of state to come to Washington in order to give him support for the nuclear deal with Iran actually sounds inspired by a plan for peace that for now is not materializing. The Quds force, a branch of Iran's Revolutionary Guards, operates with the support of Hezbollah in thirty countries on five continents. Only in 2011 were its plans discovered for a mass attack on

Washington, with the prime target being the Saudi Embassy. A new cell has recently been identified in Cyprus. It can no longer rely on anti-Sunni hatred, given that Al-Qaeda has formerly taken refuge in Tehran and Iran has given aid to Hamas. The U.S. president wanted at all costs to reiterate, despite whatever the Arab countries say about it, that Iran will play a new and more important role in the Middle East. Yet, what will Iran's role be when it has 6,000 centrifuges to enrich the uranium still in its hands and the ballistic capacity to launch an atomic weapon?

Thus, the United States today experiences a two-front crisis with its usual partners, Saudi Arabia and Egypt, one front being their alliance with the Shiites, and the other their efforts to reach out to the Muslim Brotherhood. Since 2011, when Tahrir Square gave the unequivocal signal of change, the U.S. administration hoped that the Brotherhood would prove itself a moderate force, abandoning it only when General al-Sisi's government firmly consolidated. The general is perhaps the best leader we see in the Middle East today, a man capable of choices dictated by foresight and good sense, as well as, of course, personal gain for his country. Who can fault him for the latter? His country is tormented, starved, and threatened by the Muslim Brotherhood and by ISIS in the Sinai and even in Cairo, where the Italian consulate in Cairo was attacked in July 2015.

Obama reached out to Muhammad Morsi, trusting in his democratic election… for as long as he was able to. James Clapper, U.S. Director of National Intelligence, at the time declared that the Muslim Brotherhood is a complex organization and "largely secular." The president, however, distanced himself from al-Sisi when he assumed power because the latter had overthrown a democratically elected government. This government, though, had threatened to undo the peace treaty with

Israel and was in the process of imposing Sharia law, and, on coming to power, it swiftly set up a regime of paternalistic corrupt cooptation for which all government and government-related positions, down to the last bailiff, were open only to members of the Brotherhood.

The new Egypt is now deeply involved in the battle against subversive groups, all stemming from the Brotherhood, and has outlawed Hamas in a February 2015 ruling that declared it a terrorist organization and condemned its militants for their involvement in attacks in the Sinai.

Therefore, while President al-Sisi was in fact opening a new unitary pathway in the Arab world to combat fundamentalism, the West was pulling away and suspending all military aid to Egypt.

In reality the Brotherhood has had a fundamentalist and decidedly jihadist character since its inception: Ambassador Zvi Mazel points out that among the best (so to speak) followers of bin Laden, the United States' worst enemy, we find the cornerstones of the Brotherhood. The most important names are Abdullah Azzam, bin Laden's mentor and teacher, as well as the founder of Al-Qaeda, and Muhammad Qutb, brother of Sayyid, whose teachings are the true source of modern Islamist thought. Sayyid Qutb, in fact, triggered the great Islamic revolution of today, preaching a necessary return to its origins and the attack on the West, which has callously crushed the Muslim world, according to his interpretation.

There's no branch or offshoot of global Sunni terrorism that is not tied to the Muslim Brotherhood, from Sadat's assassins in 1981 to the bombers of the World Trade Center in 1993 to the bombers of the Twin Towers in 2001 to, of course, the terrorists of Hamas. Moreover, the Brotherhood is no stranger to the bloody Sunni campaign against the Shiites in these years.

## If the Arab World Takes Control of Its Own Fate

Both the new reorganization of alliances and their self-perception of being those most directly affected by ISIS and by the agreement with Iran have pushed the Saudis and Egyptians to try to take control of the region's destiny. Both Riyadh and Cairo are, in different ways, adversaries of the Brotherhood, whom they consider a mortal enemy. The Saudis claim that their regime, in reality always caught between fundamentalism and closeness to the West, is Islam's genuine and primary expression, worthy of the leadership of the entire Muslim world and control of its holy places. However, the Muslim Brotherhood refuses to concede any legitimacy to its rulers, taking advantage of the people's discontent toward the rich and corrupt monarchy. Therefore, starting from the 2010 revolutions, Saudi Arabia opposed the Muslim Brotherhood, which not only had filled Egypt's public squares but had also subsequently taken control of its government, and went on to use its abundant economic means to help al-Sisi's revolution against the hapless Morsi.

On the international playing field, Qatar and Turkey find themselves on the opposing team. They openly endorse the Brotherhood but also underhandedly support Iran. At the same time they have a tradition of close ties with the West, so much so that Turkey is a part of NATO.

Qatar is a small, rich emirate, the brilliant inventor of the television station Al Jazeera, the Middle East's intellectual and informational long arm, dictating popular opinion in Arab homes all over. The country has just under 300,000 citizens and more than one and a half million foreigners and guest workers, and it is successfully aspiring to play a significant role both in the region and worldwide. Thanks to a clever double play, the emirate is home to the United States' military base in the Middle East, although press reports describe its substantial allocation of funds to Al-Qaeda and ISIS.

In October 2014, when the young Qatari emir Sheikh Tamim bin Hamad al-Thani was interviewed by CNN journalist Christiane Amanpour, he explained his strategy in the following manner: "I'm not in a camp against another camp. I have my own way of thinking." And his way of thinking allows him to deliver materials and money to the Muslim Brotherhood. He seems to have helped support Morsi after his election with five million dollars. In Libya he has given millions of dollars in weapons to rebels and also releases rivers of gold to be transferred to so-called Islamic "charitable institutions," which finance jihadist organizations. He also has agreements with Hezbollah and the Taliban, while in 2012 and 2013, without so much as even trying to be subtle, he provided at least 3,500 tons of weapons to rebels, including the Al-Nusra Front.

Qatar has a truly special relationship with Hamas. It has welcomed Khaled Meshal, its leader, who was hosted for years by Assad in Damascus until the current conflict forced him to flee in 2012. Between December 2014 and the beginning of 2015, it seemed that Meshal was no longer accepted by the emir and that it would be better for him to move to Turkey, where he had established excellent relations with President Erdoğan. In January 2015, however, the emir was quick to refute these rumors. Doha is very generous with him, and the flow of millions that they give him ends up fomenting Hamas's ballistic supply, all under the guise of aid to the population of Gaza and to building the notorious tunnels used by its terrorists.

Some White House advisors have suggested to Obama that he relocate the U.S. military base elsewhere, but for now the president has not yet made a decision. According to an analysis spread by the Arab world to the chancelleries of much of the Western world, the terrorist threat is unrelated to Islam, but rather, as the emir of Qatar says, "The problem isn't Islam—it's hopelessness…that abounds in the Syrian and Palestinian refugee camps, and in war-weary towns and villages in Syria, Iraq, Yemen, Libya, and Gaza. It's the hopelessness we see in the poorer neighborhoods of Europe's great cities, and, yes, even the United States."

The analysis of terrorism as a social and not ideological phenomenon is widely accepted. Even President Obama maintains this view: "What's true, though, is that when millions of people—especially youth—are impoverished and have no hope for the future, when corruption inflicts daily humiliations on people, the risk of instability and extremism grow.… And terrorist groups are all too happy to step into a void. They try to justify their violence in the name of fighting the injustice of corruption…even while those terrorist groups end up committing even worse abuses."

It is true that the element of Middle Eastern poverty plays its role, and it is always desirable, even virtuous, to want increased prosperity for a population that suffers. Yet to set up plans to battle terrorism without identifying its source doesn't help those who see firsthand today that their enemy receives aid and sympathy in a competition that is made of dynamite and blood, like Saudi Arabia, for example, which has funded terrorism for decades.

The relationship between the United States and Turkey has also brought pause to both Egypt and Saudi Arabia: Islamism and Erdoğan's Ottoman ambitions now make Turkey a strong and ambivalent contender in Middle East strategy, just like Qatar.

It's sufficient to consider how Ankara, which is Assad's mortal enemy (his father financed the Kurds of the PKK), had forged Machiavellian alliances with the Assad regime shortly before the revolution in Syria in the new hegemonic vision of an Islamic Middle East headed by Turkey. Now, while it allies itself with Hezbollah Shiites and ISIS threatens its border, it gives free reign to the passage of foreign fighters headed to Syria and Iraq and covertly aids the caliphate despite being a member of NATO—though it has lately used its bombers to strike some of ISIS's positions.

Thus the foreign fighters who intend to go to Syria usually book a one-way ticket to Ankara and proceed undisturbed on their way to joining ISIS's army.

Ankara carries out a very active international policy. It openly declares its sympathy for Hamas: the epitome of its many friendly gestures was the notorious Freedom Flotilla, deployed by the Turkish organization IHH, tied to the Muslim Brotherhood, which, while claiming to deliver humanitarian aid, on May 31, 2010, headed for Gaza's coast. Erdoğan's anti-Semitic tirades went so far as to call Shimon Peres an assassin at the Davos Conference in 2009, shellacking Israel with insults and threats of war whenever he had the chance (and sometimes when he wasn't even given the chance). Turkey not only supports the Islamists in Libya who have made Tripoli their capital against the Tobruk regime, backed by Egypt, but has also been accused of providing weapons to ISIS and Al-Qaeda fighting in the area. In April 2015, a Turkish cargo ship was shelled so that, as the Tobruk regime stated, it couldn't arrive to deliver a deadly shipload to its fundamentalist friends. Erdoğan follows the same strategy as Qatar, that is, he sits back, fraternizing with the Brotherhood, and enjoys America's backing, which he has never been without, despite his favorable attitude toward Hamas and ISIS, or his aggressive anti-Egyptian politics.

Erdoğan's double-dealing is refined. He is open about his ultimate goal, the restoration of the Ottoman Empire, and is opposed to a policy of Islamist repression domestically. While helping ISIS, he forces an entry into Syria and confronts Assad's forces in order to reclaim control of a shrine of the Ottoman

Empire in the province of Aleppo (the tomb of Suleyman Shah, the grandfather of the founder of the empire). He makes visits to Tehran and is friends with Putin; he reiterates that Israel must disappear, but he has ambitions to join the EU; he argues that the deposition of Morsi is the result of a conspiracy of the American Zionist lobby, but he remains an important member of NATO.

On the one hand, Turkey acts in such a way as to qualify itself as a leader of the anti-Western camp, and on the other it maintains good relations with the United States. Furthermore, with its current position it contributes to the formulation of new types of alliances that are completely different than those that now exist. With the latter aim in mind, Turkey has started to build convenient relations for the near future in order to find a way of getting out of the hysterical crisis of the Middle East caused by the grip of the caliph and the ayatollah.

## A New Middle East is Possible

During Operation Protective Edge in 2014, the Saudis shared with al-Sisi, who was its promoter, a distinctly anti-Hamas policy. Riyadh had financed Hamas until 2005, the year in which the Palestinian organization allied with Iran, despite it being a Shiite state, which angered the Saudis. In recent years, the latter had fought against both the Muslim Brotherhood and Iran. However, a new event meant that it was time for them to flex a little muscle. In this way, what would come to be known as the "Arab NATO" was formed in order to advance against the Houthi, Iran's allies, who conquered most of Yemen while the United States was starting negotiations with the republic of the ayatollahs.

Saudi Arabia began bombing the Houthi in Yemen on March 26, 2015, announcing the formation of a military coalition with the participation of Egypt, Jordan, Morocco, the United Arab Emirates, Kuwait, Qatar, Bahrain, and even Sudan. The president of Yemen had asked for a military intervention. Obviously, Iran condemned the operation, while all accused it of funding the rebels, and even John Kerry asked the Islamic regime to stop arming them. Only the European Union, Russia, and the United Nations have criticized that which, instead, could be considered the Arab world's greatest regional initiative to bring order to the chaos into which it has sunk.

It is interesting to hear what pro-Western and anti-Hezbollah Lebanese Interior Minister Nohad El Machnouk asserted immediately after the negotiations with Iran began: "There will be an Arab awakening: In the end, it turns out there are Arabs who decided they will not be weak," referring to the Saudi-led campaign in Yemen. They will understand, he continued, that "we can decide without the Americans, with or without their approval."

Meanwhile, Egypt—companion at this stage of the Saudis and the Gulf states, which were affected by the United States' choice to favor their institutional enemy, Iran—held off the Sunni extremists of Al-Qaeda and ISIS, now classified as enemies infesting the Sinai, with an armed intervention beyond its own borders. Al-Sisi's Egypt fought them hard, even making Hamas's men vacate positions from which they could infiltrate from Gaza. Al-Sisi also directed a massive military campaign against enemies who, from Libya, along a dangerous border, extensive and rugged, threatened the Land of the Pharaohs.

You cannot help but notice how, in the same period, with silent but decisive work, Israel has operated in the same direction: with several targeted attacks, it has hit the patrols and supplies of joint weapons between Syrian and Lebanese Hezbollah fighters along the Syrian-Lebanon border—by now one border really—identifying the new and widespread Iranian presence on that border as the real enemy. Meanwhile, however, Israel has not neglected to curtail the continuous terrorist attacks by Hamas and other formations, in addition to hunting down young Palestinian foreign fighters on its territory who are returning from Syria or ready to join ISIS, or aggressive cells and lone terrorists, always Sunnis, who are part of the growing Islamist movement among Palestinians and Israeli Arabs. During and after the military operation in Gaza in 2014, the movement had organized various demonstrations in northern Israel and the Palestinian territories calling for the destruction of Israel, "Jerusalem's liberation," and waving ISIS flags.

So, we have two big Arab powers, Saudi Arabia and Egypt, of course dissimilar and, in the past, often at odds with each other, and the Gulf States that are now realizing that they must defend themselves against new threats in an international situation in which the United States assumes a different role from the one it played in the past.

The riskiest consequence of America's abandonment of the old Sunni alliance is a looming dreadful prospect. Iran remains in possession of more than 6,000 centrifuges and continues to work on a ballistic missile program, and it doesn't intend to budge on this. Moreover, it is not yet clear whether the Atomic Energy Agency will monitor the Iranian nuclear centers based on an agreement with many secret stipulations, which, in any case, is only in force for a decade. In short, Iran remains a nuclear threat because the only thing certain in this intricate agreement is a statement by Tehran that it will allow inspectors to visit military facilities in the country only on the conditions already mentioned (i.e., 24-days notice and the eventual establishment of a joint committee). Also, let's not forget the Republic of Iran's "moral obligation" to destroy Israel, "non-negotiable," as Muhammad Reza Naqdi, commander of the *basij* militia, stated in March 2015, at the height of the negotiations!

We can ascertain the consequences of a nuclear Iran in a statement by Saudi Prince Turki bin Faisal, a former intelligence chief and ambassador to Washington, in which he said: "We can't sit back and be nowhere as Iran is allowed to retain much of its capability [of uranium enrichment] and amass its research [on enriched uranium]." He continued: "Whatever the Iranians have, we will have, too," that is to say, "[The deal] opens the door to nuclear proliferation." Not only this, but the suspension of sanctions will bring into Iran's state coffers around $150 billion within a year.

In the view of the Sunni countries, there is no doubt that Iran is lying. Given that the Islamic world is more capable than us of devising a long-term policy and of imagining the international arena as a stage for their future exploits, they are now engaged in redesigning their future political relations. They see, therefore, a possible ally in Putin and have demonstrated this hope through various meetings, such as the one between al-Sisi and the Russian leader. These meetings have been immediately fruitful, bringing economic aid and many business opportunities, despite the former Soviet Union's friendship with Iran. They also see China and India as two parties that can replace the uncertain American friend.

In August 2014, al-Sisi visited Moscow and discussed with Putin a military deal worth three billion dollars, which also involves Saudi Arabia and the United Arab Emirates. After a small disagreement on Riyadh's military campaign, which Putin had criticized, sparking the ire of the Saudi king, Russia, historically Iran's ally, tried to mend relations by inviting King Abdullah to Moscow.

Once it became clear that an agreement with Iran was at hand, al-Sisi wasted no time with recriminations and sought new alliances. In December 2014, Egypt and China signed a series of strategic agreements in various areas, not just military.

China will invest in Egypt's infrastructure, particularly in renewable energy, as well as in tourism, and it will favor the importation of Egyptian products. Al-Sisi believes that in this manner he can not only diversify his country's arms suppliers but also obtain more investments into its economy.

In general, the interests of the Sunni Arab countries, especially those of Saudi Arabia and Egypt, are very close to those of Israel, whatever the ideological perception of the Jewish state may be. Certainly, Israel remains a presence full of challenges for any regime in the region, particularly because of its standard of living, which is much higher than that of the Arab world, as well as the technological, agricultural, scientific, and cultural development it has achieved despite being in a continuous state of war. The onset of new common strategic interests, however, can be considered a possible opportunity for a future in which the countries of the region look at Israel's technological, economic, and social capabilities with less hostility, and perhaps even draw benefits from them.

This will certainly be an uphill battle because there persists a very heavy theological abuse of power toward Jews and the Jewish state—a nation that finds itself on lands considered part of the Muslim *umma*.

## Alliances Based on Shared Interests

We cannot, therefore, depend on an organic alliance to provide a turning point in the Middle East. Rather, we must depend on a series of strategic moves that are convenient for all those who have an interest in fighting the wave of savage terrorism underway and in opposing Iran's hegemonic ambitions. It is no coincidence that there was much grumbling about Saudi Arabia's secret proposals to leave their airspace open for any Israeli incursions into Iran. But this remains in the realm of media embellishments. What is certain, on the other hand, and caused much buzz, was a meeting at the beginning of June 2015 in Washington that included the Director-General of the Israel Ministry of Foreign Affairs, Dore Gold, and the Saudi government advisor Anwar Majed Eshki. They shook hands in public and discussed the Iranian threat. In the past six months, the Saudis and Israelis have met in secret at least five times.

At present, we can consider the strategic interests of a large part of the Arab world as an open road for a "peace process," to use the term that has been conventionally applied for years. In order for it to truly occur, common interests must dictate it. Additionally, the Palestinians must be in a position to find it useful to integrate themselves rather than representing the eternal, unfailing source of discord in the region. So far in this role they have found aid, and benefits, and even Hamas has participated in the party. Now everything could change: the shower of aid could come not in exchange for the Israeli–Palestinian conflict, but in exchange for a role in the battle against terrorism and an atmosphere of tranquility, which could be inspired by Abu Mazen's return to the negotiating table.

History, today, puts much of the Arab world, including the Palestinians, on the same side with Israel and the West, that is, against terrorism. The Arab states, Israel, and Western countries are all caught in the grip between the caliph and the ayatollah, and they could get out of it together if they reach an agreement that allows these ancient enemies to coexist, even if they don't love each other.

This could give us some respite, at least for some time, from the great anger of these past few years, that anger which has led to nuclear aspirations and an imperialist policy on the one side, and an unprecedented explosion of violence on the other, a violence that has beheaded American journalists, burned a

Jordanian pilot alive, and smashed the masterpieces of Palmyra to smithereens.

Whether you like him or not in relation to his management of power, which is certainly very tough and sometimes dictatorial, al-Sisi is the promoter of an anti-jihadist reaction within the Islamic world, and the only one calling for bold reform of his clergy. He touched on this on January 1, 2015, when speaking at Al-Azhar University, the most important center of Islamic studies. "I am referring here to the religious clerics. We have to think hard about what we are facing. It is inconceivable that the thinking that we hold most sacred should cause the entire *umma* [Islamic nation] to be a source of anxiety, danger, killing, and destruction for the rest of the world. That thinking [*fikr*]—I am not saying religion [*din*]—that corpus of texts and ideas that we have held sacred over the years, to the point that departing from them has become almost impossible, is antagonizing the entire world! Is it possible that 1.6 billion people should want to kill the rest of the world's inhabitants—that is 7 billion—so that they themselves may live? Impossible. I am saying these words here at Al-Azhar, before this assembly of scholars and *ulema* [learned men]—All this that I am telling you, you cannot feel it if you remain trapped within this mindset. You need to step outside of yourselves to be able to observe it and reflect on it from a more enlightened perspective.... We are in need of a religious revolution. You imams are responsible before Allah. The entire world, I say it again, the entire world is waiting for your next move … because this *umma* is being torn, it is being destroyed, it is being lost—and it is being lost by our own hands."

Al-Sisi was ready to recognize Islam's responsibility and to call for its reform in the face of the danger that confronts it; the Saudis and their neighbors have stopped funding the Brotherhood and ceased playing with the fire of terror when they turned against it. Al-Sisi said that the religious are "responsible for bringing the religious discourse in harmony with the spirit of the times." A courageous and far-sighted argument, since it calls upon the jurists and religious authorities to reform Islam from within.

The failed attempts to impose forms of government and social structures valid to the West have demonstrated one thing, which Bernard Lewis has continuously repeated: the solution to the crisis of Islam must grow within Islam. Democracy has been rejected as a poisonous Western dish eaten only by the powerful, leaving the people to starve. However, while the Islamists were preparing their war against the West, no one thought that the sea of violence produced within the schools of Islamic thought might overwhelm the entire Muslim world.

In the chaos, however, history is showing us a path to follow, perhaps the only one for now, and certainly the best: to form an alliance with the Sunni Arab world against Iran and ISIS. This alliance would not represent an intellectual inclination to Wahhabi Saudi Arabia, which applies Sharia law to the letter. Nor is it a loving relationship with al-Sisi's Egypt, which is in part a military dictatorship. It is an agreement to build on common interests and solid goals, which are those of bringing a new balance to the Middle East, freeing us from the threat posed by Iran and from the danger of global jihadism.

Piecing together this alliance would also mean giving power, strength, and support to those within the Arab world who want a different Islam. It could give them courage. For that to happen, one cannot just declare war on the Muslim Brotherhood and lock them in jail. One must call for the involvement of those who the traditional authority renders credible in the eyes of the people, such as the sheikhs, jurists, sages, and commenters, those people who are able to reform Islam from within. Al-Sisi is attempting precisely this.

History presents us with a unique opportunity, but it takes the courage of a true leader and the depth of a religious reformer to encourage this process, to restore the West on the path toward peace and prosperity that it vowed to embrace after the Second World War.

Paradoxically, the histories of the Middle East and relations between the Western world and Islam have never proved so open to a breakthrough as they are now. The game is not played only in the field of Islamic states. We in the West, too, now more than ever, are interested in working for peace in that area. In other words, beyond just welcoming citizens from those countries of the Middle East and Africa that are opposed to Islamic extremism, we must stand side by side with them. Such a thing is not easy for us because it means a double commitment, both at home and in the places of origin of these refugees. The economy must overcome its selfishness, but generosity must also be regulated in accordance with the wealth of one's own country. The purpose of this is not to flaunt our own moral dignity by stating, "See? I'm so good." The temptation is strong, but it would be better to state, "I have thought about our children, as well as your own."

It is clear that as long as the Middle East and Africa remain infested by Islamist imperialism, they will continue to produce a tide of desperate people fleeing toward Europe. Those choosing to escape will only increase in number, not decrease, with the "refugees welcome" policy that Angela Merkel has inaugurated. Therefore, in order to avoid an increase in the number of refugees in Europe while still preserving this open-door policy, it is manifest that aid needs to be transferred to the countries of origin. This will require investing in economic structures, in education, in construction…a huge number of undertakings, much bigger than what we can imagine from the comfortable view of our Western home. Moreover, this investment can yield a fruitful outcome if it is coupled with a local commitment, especially if this commitment helps hit the enemy and neutralize its power. In short, European policy can set in motion a virtuous cycle, but only if doesn't stop at solely accepting refugees and doing nothing more.

This is also essential for Europe. The cascade of immigration into the EU can create a popular backlash that runs the risk of transforming sense of identity into racism, fear of foreigners into violence, and jealousy over assistance into political apathy. Welcoming refugees, if not accompanied by effective integration policies, can become a springboard for movements of the extreme right and, on the other hand, can allow jihadism to flourish, which will certainly arrive with the refugees who belong to fleeing factions.

It is therefore necessary for Europe to succeed in promoting the desire of these newcomers to become German, Italian, French, etc. We know that for now at least the integration process exhibits many flaws, especially among the younger generations from which foreign fighters and neo-jihadist movements originate. A cautious distribution of the workforce will be essential. It is true that Europe, with a growth rate of only 1.6 percent, is eager for foreign labor, but then its economic crisis forces it to protect whatever it has and to act with hostility toward whoever comes to live off its resources.

On the other hand, in the countries of origin of these refugees, they study from childhood onward a fantasy dogma that blames the West for all the troubles of Africa and the Middle East. It will not be easy to keep this from becoming a cultural substrate among the new immigrants.

There is a lot to do. The protagonists are still the moderate Sunni countries, the lifeline for the whole world once they oppose jihadist war for their own interests. Their alliance with Europe must be firm and active, as their future is also contingent on economic, social, and political renewal. The upheavals in Europe affect them as well.

Egypt, Saudi Arabia, Gulf countries…everybody can be part of the solution. Perhaps even Qatar, despite what we have said, may be interested in helping to calm the waters with its immense wealth. Only Sunni and Shiite extremism can take advantage of the confusion, and only multiple actions created by the dramatic convergence of interests may mitigate or stop the wave.

The words uttered by Kinan Masalmeh, a Syrian child, were so sensible. Breaking the tide of pietistic observations that accompanied his journey, he told reporters, "Just stop the war. We don't want to go to Europe." Sure, it's difficult. Beyond just goodwill, weapons are needed to halt the other weapons, and a lot of money must be spent to restore a livable reality. The road of common interests brings, along with a sense of vertigo, a plan for a future in which the good guys, or semi-good, or false good, create a united front against the bad guys for at least a short while. We have to hope this time as well. We have to hope again.

# Bibliography

To FACILITATE THE READING of this book and in order to avoid weighing down the text, I have chosen not to insert footnotes and references in individual chapters. I propose here some books, as well as news articles and commentaries—certainly not all of them that have accumulated over the years on my desk but some of the most important—that I have used in the writing of this book.

First of all, to understand what is happening today, some fundamental studies on the Middle East, Islam, and terrorism are necessary.

In order to comprehend the contemporary Middle East, books by the great Middle East historian, and my teacher, Bernard Lewis, are essential. Lewis was the first to define a scientific, historical, and cultural methodology in the field of Middle Eastern studies and has been able to predict and confront for some time many of the crises of Islam. Two vital texts on Middle East history, Islam, and Muslims are *The Shaping of the Modern Middle East* (Oxford University Press, 1994) and *Islam: The Religion and the People*, co-authored with Buntzie Churchill (FT Press, 2008). Among the various studies on the relationship between the West and Islam, see *The Muslim Discovery of Europe* (W. W. Norton & Company, 2001).

Bernard Lewis was the first to study political Islam and the conflicting relationship between Islam and Western modernity.

Among his most important works is *The Political Language of Islam* (University of Chicago Press, 1991), which analyzes Islamic political concepts and their mistranslation into Western ones. In *What Went Wrong? Western Impact and Middle Eastern Response* (Oxford University Press, 2002), Lewis examines the origins of the clash between the West and the Middle East by providing the first comprehensive analysis of political Islam, which he then elaborated upon in *The Crisis of Islam: Holy War and Unholy Terror* (Random House, 2004).

To understand the relationship between the West and Islam, and especially the Western world's submissive attitude, Bat Ye'or's studies were the first to give a name to describe the subjugation of Europe—*dhimmitude*. See *Islam and Dhimmitude: Where Civilizations Collide* (Fairleigh Dickinson University Press, 2001). In addition to being the first to talk about *dhimmitude*, Bat Ye'or has pioneered studies on the Islamization of Europe by carefully studying its pro-Arab policy. See *Eurabia: The Euro-Arab Axis* (Fairleigh Dickinson University Press, 2005). For a summary of her work, see the author's last book *Comprendere Eurabia: L'inarrestabile islamizzazione dell'Europa* (Lindau, 2015).

Europe's capitulation to Islam is accompanied by a general attitude on the continent that, as Oriana Fallaci denounces, has lost all sense. On the blindness of the multiculturalists and their paralysis in the face of terrorism, see her books *The Rage and the Pride* (Rizzoli, 2002) and *The Force of Reason* (Rizzoli, 2004). Melanie Phillips has written on the same subject. See her book *The World Turned Upside Down* (Encounter Books, 2011). On the relationship between Europe and Israel, as well as on how anti-Semitism is justified with human rights arguments, I would like to recommend my book *Gli antisemiti progressisti* (Rizzoli, 2004), which I wrote in order to document the incredible reactions to Europe's first big wave of suicide terrorism against Israel. In addition, see my book *Israele siamo noi* (Rizzoli, 2007), in which I formulate the thesis that Israel, although threatened by suicide terrorism and by accusations of pseudo-pacifists, actually represents all of us in the West. On how Israel has become the accused *par excellence*, the pariah of nations, see Robin Shepherd's *A State Beyond the Pale: Europe's Problem with Israel* (Orion Publishing, 2009), which analyzes chapter by chapter what he describes as a real disease. In relation to the UN, beyond the millions of articles, its dyscrasias are well explained, along with the hypocrisy of the international community in relation to human rights and the Islamic world, in Dore Gold's *Tower of Babble: How the United Nations has Fueled Global Chaos* (Crown Forum, 2005). See also the excellent work Gerald Steinberg has done on NGOs and their contributions to the same chaos.

As for studies on terrorism, its development in the contemporary world, and its threats to our civilization, see the great classics by the historian Walter Laqueur, *Terrorism* (Little, Brown & Company, 1977), *The Age of Terrorism* (Little, Brown & Company, 1987), *The New Terrorism: Fanaticism and the Arms of Mass Destruction* (Oxford University Press, 1999), and *No End to War: Terrorism in the Twenty-First Century* (Continuum International Publishing Group, 2003), as well as the analyses in *Post-Modern Terrorism: Trends, Scenarios, and Future Threats*, published by the International Institute for Counter Terrorism (ICT) at the Interdisciplinary Center Herzliya, Israel, in 2006. Furthermore, I have always particularly liked Paul Berman's *Terror and Liberalism* (W. W. Norton & Company, 2003), which brings a new perspective on Islamist terrorism by comparing it to twentieth-century totalitarianisms and arguing that Islamism is its contemporary form.

On the origin and structure of ISIS, among the by now many books available, see Maurizio Molinari, *Il califfato del terrore: Perché lo Stato Islamico minaccia l'Occidente* (Rizzoli, 2015); Domenico Quirico, *Il grande califfato* (Neri Pozza, 2015); and Loretta Napoleoni, *Isis: Lo Stato del terrore* (Feltrinelli, 2015). In addition, see the Italian periodical *Limes*, no. 3 (2015), entitled "Chi ha paura del califfo." Also very interesting is the book of my late friend Khaled Fouad Allam, *Il jihadista della porta accanto* (Piemme, 2014), and very stimulating—as always—is Carlo Panella's *Il libro nero del califfato* (Rizzoli, 2015).

There are also endless articles. Here is a brief selection:

On the birth and development of ISIS, see Hussain Abdul-Hussain and Lee Smith, "On the Origin of ISIS: Why Has a Terrorist State Blossomed in Syria and Iraq?," *Weekly Standard*, vol. 19, no. 48, September 8, 2014.

On the first decisive battles by ISIS for territorial expansion, see Jonathan Spyer, "Islamic State Fighters Are Moving Ever Closer towards Israel," *Jerusalem Post*, December 27, 2014. Also, see the many reports and analyses by Aymenn Jawad Al-Tamimi on his website, http://www.aymennjawad.org.

On support for ISIS, see David Pollock, "What Do People in the Middle East Think about the Islamic State? These Poll Results Will Surprise You," *New Republic*, October 16, 2014.

On the large outpouring of volunteers from all over the world who have left to join ISIS, see Swati Sharma "Map: How the Flow of Foreign Fighters to Iraq and Syria Has Surged since October," *Washington Post*, January 27, 2015. See also the article by Soeren Kern "European Jihadists in Syria," published by the Gatestone Institute, January 23, 2014.

In particular, on the recruitment of women and their role in ISIS, read Ben Winsor, "ISIS Is Actively Recruiting Female Fighters to Brutalize Other Women," *Business Insider*, October 14, 2014, and Shiv Malik, "Lured by ISIS: How the Young

Girls Who Revel in Brutality Are Offered Cause," *Guardian*, February 21, 2015. In addition, see Homa Khaleeli, "Domestic Terrorism: Isis Housewives Told How to Prepare Battle Snacks," *Guardian*, November 5, 2014.

On ISIS's ideology and strategy—and especially for its excellent proof in relation to the undeniable connection between ISIS and textual Islam—see the analysis by Graeme Wood, "What ISIS Really Wants," *Atlantic*, March 2015.

On ISIS's atrocities, see Ben Winsor, "This Might Be the Most Horrific Atrocity ISIS Has Committed," *Business Insider*, October 30, 2014.

In contrast to studies on Islam and on the danger posed by ISIS, the literature on contemporary Iran is not very evolved and must be obtained from general texts on the Middle East, like those of Bernard Lewis, or those on terrorism. One of the most fundamental books on the subject, however, is Dore Gold's *The Rise of Nuclear Iran: How Tehran Defies the West* (Regnery Publishing, 2009). Useful analyses published according to changes in the situation can also be obtained from the Jerusalem Center for Public Affairs. Among the latter, particularly in the series *Strategic Perspectives*, see Harold Rhode, *The Source of Iranian Negotiating Behavior*. Other important articles include: Manda Zand Ervin, "The Mullahs and the Real Iran," *American Thinker*, April 30, 2015; and Benjamin Weinthal, "To Confront Iran's Jingoism and Domestic Repression, Change Its Regime," *Jerusalem Post*, March 29, 2015. For a commentary on Iranian culture, see Harold Rhode's chapter in *Identity Crisis in Iran: Politics, Culture, and Religion* (Lexington Books, 2015), especially the chapter entitled, "The Unending Battle Between the Persian and the Islamic Identities." See also issue no. 114 of *Middle East Security and Policy Studies*, published by the Begin-Sadat Center for Strategic Studies in 2015, particularly Yossi Kuperwasser's paper, "Israel's Role in the Struggle over the Iranian Nuclear Project."

On Obama's policy in the Middle East, there is a new article every day, particularly with regard to his administration's agreement with Iran. See, for example, Max Boot, "Obama's Mideast Realignment," *Wall Street Journal*, March 25, 2015; and Bradley Klapper, "Iran Is at the Center of Obama's Complicated Middle East Policy," *Business Insider*, March 27, 2015. Also very interesting is Michael Oren, *Ally: My Journey Across the American-Israeli Divide* (Penguin Random House, 2015).

Finally, on the common interests that are being created and the possibility of a new Middle East, there are countless newspaper articles. I readily recommend any by Dan Diker and Harold Rhode in the *Jerusalem Post*. See also Jay Solomon and Ahmed Al Omran, "Saudi Nuclear Deal Raises Stakes for Iran Talks," *Wall Street Journal*, March 11, 2015; and Yaron Friedman, "Al-Sisi's Peace Plan," *Ynet*, November 26, 2014.

# Acknowledgements

I wish to extend my thanks to Dr. Giovanni Matteo Quer and Dr. Tommaso Virgili. Their research experience and in-depth academic knowledge of the Middle East and Europe have made them indispensable interlocutors.

www.ingramcontent.com/pod-product-compliance
Lightning Source LLC
Chambersburg PA
CBHW070121260726
48658CB00001B/203